From Sugarcane to Surrey

Palewell Press

From Sugarcane to Surrey

A tale of despair, humiliation and hope

Jay Woogara

From Sugarcane to Surrey
First edition 2023 from Palewell Press,
https://palewellpress.co.uk
Printed and bound in the UK
ISBN 978-1-911587-70-5

A CIP catalogue record for this title is available from the British Library.

Dedication

This book is dedicated to my Dadi (paternal grandmother) who nurtured me selflessly.

Happy and sad childhood memories
Torment me incessantly.
They crowd my thoughts at once,
Yet I keep coming back to one.

I am at home with my dear Dadi,
Lying with my head on her shoulder,
On a stuffed mattress on our cow dung floor,
Sharing what we have with our cow Ramu.

'Look at those flashing stars beta,'
My Dadi shouts with delight
Pointing at them with her walking stick
Her bony hands hugging me tighter.

How beautiful they looked,
Twinkling and beckoning
Me to leave,
Through the holes in the thatch.

I stared at the stars,
I prayed and wished,
'Please, take me away to the land of plenty,'
With my Dadi always besides me.

Contents

Chapter One

I do not recall ever playing with my Papa. He was only forty-eight years old when he died, I was not even four. It grieves me enormously that I did not get the opportunity to know him as a person. My family does not possess a single photograph of him. When he was alive, neither my family nor any of the other villagers on our road had any sort of camera with which to capture images. Our only priority in life was to survive. Ma had to provide for four children, all under ten years old; our Dadi my paternal grandmother and, of course, my Papa who never worked for others.

Our village was in the northern part of Mauritius, and the summer of 1948, like every other, was very hot. My mother was away in the forest searching for the best fodder for our cow, Ramu, and her three precious goats. Dadi wrapped in her torn sari, was at home looking after me. I was roaming about on the muddy road in front of our sugarcane thatched house, bare-footed and wearing my torn, dirty shorts, when an out-of-breath Creole man came galloping towards me. He was tall and black with curly hair. I was terrified of Creoles. I thought they were alien because they spoke a completely different language. I could only converse in Bhojpuri, a Hindi dialect. I rushed to my Dadi, He followed me to our yard, breathless, the sweat dripping from his forehead.

'Dadi, Dadi, a Creole is chasing me'.

I ran like a rabbit and hid behind her sari.

‘Madame Woogara, Madame Woogara. I’m Jean, the fisherman, a friend of your son,’ he kept saying in Creole between bouts of panting. But he could not make my Dadi understand. The only part Dadi could decipher was ‘ton garçon’. In the end, with the help of a neighbour and lots of arm waving, the fisherman managed to communicate to Dadi that my Papa was seriously ill on the beach at Trou aux Biches.

Panic broke out. Dadi started yelling, and soon my three siblings and Dadi started running after the fisherman, followed by at least five villagers. Nobody thought about me; I was left behind.

Trou aux Biches is at least a mile away from our village, and a good thirty minutes walking at a rapid pace. I was determined to join the crowd and thought it was great game until I was firmly grabbed by a chachee. In the village all women who were not related were known as chachees. The male elders were called chachas.

I was with the neighbour when Ma arrived home. She had already been filled in by the villagers and looked very agitated. Despite the terrible news, Ma managed to feed the cow and the goats and left water for the animals. Accompanied by a neighbour, Ma and I ran all the way to the seaside where we found my Papa lying stretched out and motionless on the white sand. Dadi was holding his head in her lap and crying and praying to God. Ma rushed to him with both her hands rapidly tapping her chest and yelling very loudly. I held my Papa’s hands. They were cold. My Papa was dead.

Jean told Ma that Papa fell from the boat of a fisherman and drowned. The fisherman, being the sole person on the boat had difficulty rescuing him. In the end he managed to drag him back into the boat and brought him to the shore. Ma and Dadi thought his death was mysterious.

With the help of the fishermen and the villagers my Papa, clad in his white dhoti, was carried to the shade of a coconut tree.

While my three siblings and some of the village women were still crying, I stood clutching the hand of Dadi who, with Ma, stood motionless, sobbing and staring at the corpse of Papa. Two police officers and a doctor were standing nearby, deep in conversation with each other. One of our chachas explained to Dadi that my Papa's body had to be transported to the hospital to determine the cause of his death. Dadi was furious at this proposal. She wanted Papa's body at home, but she was overruled by the police officers.

Papa was taken to the nearest hospital, which was in Port Louis, in a white hospital van. After three days of anxious waiting, Papa's body was released for cremation.

According to Hindu traditions and culture, a body must be cremated within forty-eight hours. But my Papa had to wait for nearly five days to be cremated. Three men carefully washed his body and dressed him in a clean white dhoti with a pugree on his head. He was placed on our only sugarcane leaf mattress with his head to the north and his toes to the south to ensure that any remaining energy from his body was removed by the magnetic field in the north. The village men built a bamboo open coffin, while I, my siblings and some of the village boys adorned the makeshift coffin with flowers and coconut leaves.

All of us, including many villagers and our cousins sat by the body of Papa. We did not sleep at all that night. The women sang tuneless religious mantras with repetitive rhythms while the men sat outside playing cards (and probably smoking ganja). I could not work out why everybody was making such a fuss of me. Being the youngest of the family, every solemn-faced villager stroked my cheeks with their hard, crusty hands. I remained seated in the lap of my Dadi and tried very hard to console her, but my attempts seemed to fuel her shrieks. Ma and Dadi cried and hugged each other nearly all night.

The next day, following a short puja by the local pundit, the coffin was carried away to the village central cremation site on the shoulders of some of the men. They were followed by most of the male villagers. The pundit and my nine-year-old brother, the principal mourner, led the group. Dadi clutched my left hand, ensuring I stayed behind. I could not understand why I was not allowed to join the cortège with my brother. Equally none of the women were allowed to join. They just stood there amidst cries and buckets of tears until the coffin disappeared from our view. I did not realise then that my Papa would never return home again and that it would be the last time I would ever see him.

Chapter Two

I was reminded frequently that I was a fatherless little boy. My siblings were equally taunted by the village children. I recall the day when I was walking home with my brother Hemsingh, who was five years older than I, and we were approached by three boys.

'Hey, Hemsingh, where is your ganja Papa?' the taller boy shouted.

My brother stopped in his stride and glared at him. We were outnumbered, of course, but my brother was so angry he confronted the boy and hit him. The other two boys joined in, and during the fight my brother was badly beaten.

I did not understand what 'ganja Papa' meant so I asked my brother to elaborate, but he remained silent. That evening, when I asked my Dadi, she too refused to enlighten me. In fact, I was warned I must never mention the word 'ganja' again to anybody.

I missed my Papa very much, although I hardly knew him. Most of the boys in the neighbourhood had both parents. I felt sorry for myself when I saw my friend Siam was going to the sugarcane fields with his Papa, talking and laughing. But sometimes I was relieved I did not have a Papa, as more often than not I would see my friends getting beaten with long wooden sticks by their fathers. Nearly all the men in the village, being labourers, came home drunk. Perhaps, that was the only avenue for them to relax, as there was no other form of entertainment in the village. At dusk, the distant sound of slurred voices could be heard demanding a certain type of food that had not been prepared or complaining that the food was not already plated for them as soon as they walked into the house.

I often sat down under our mango tree and thought about the father I could not remember, no matter how hard I tried. I thought about his features and wondered whether he ever played with me or shouted or even beat me. But for months the only features of my Papa that appeared were his dead face and his cold hands.

My Papa's name was Jagdeo. I can only reflect about him through the words of others. One particular distant relative knew my Papa quite well as they were at primary school together. His name was Chacha Motilal. He would sell gateau piments (chilli dhal fritters) at the crossroads in the village of Trois Boutiques. Chacha Motilal was a short man with very fair skin. He had a bubbly personality and always wore a broad smile. When I was young, he wore a white dhoti, but by the time I was fifteen he had started donning brown trousers and a white shirt. I do not remember when this transformation happened, but by degrees most of the men in the village rejected Indian attire. The Creoles, who were the descendants of the first African slaves of the French, were favoured in every aspect of life then. These Creoles would laugh at the Indians because of the way they were dressed. They would call us coolies' children. It is more than likely that the villagers could not take the humiliation any longer and gradually shed their dhotis and started dressing like westerners, to impress the white farmers.

Ma and Dadi were always very reluctant to talk about my Papa and therefore it was impossible for me to glean anything about him through them. Every time I asked Dadi about my Papa she stopped in her tracks, adopted a sombre mood and failed to give me any answer on the subject. I was baffled by the adoption of such an indifferent attitude towards him.

'What was Papa like when I was a little boy?' I often asked my mother. The reply was always the same:

'I shall tell you one day. But today I am very busy.'

So, having tried every avenue to explore the life of my Papa from Ma and Dadi, I at last gave up because they even refused to mention his name.

It must have been when I was seventeen years old that I was sitting at the back of a noisy bus travelling from Port Louis to Triolet and when I noticed Chacha Motilal in the front seat. I had not seen him for many years, as at that time I had started living in Port Louis with my sister and brother-in-law. I made my way to the front seat and sat by him.

'Namaste, Chachaji,' I greeted him formally with a broad smile. Greeting an Elder in this manner was the norm in those days; otherwise, you would be seen as being disrespectful. No matter how busy one might be extra effort was required to show one's respect to them at all times. Following a preliminary enquiry, I asked Chacha Motilal about his friendship with my Papa.

'Your Papa was a gentleman, Jaysingh. I never saw him dressed in tatters. As a school friend he was very generous towards me. He was good in most subjects. English was his favourite. Do you know only three people passed the Primary School Examination and he was one of them in Triolet? I failed because I was not very clever. Your Papa would teach me Arithmetic and Hindi. I passed these two subjects but failed English and British History.'

According to Chacha Motilal, Papa was a pleasant person and one of his main weaknesses was his generosity. He could have become a government school teacher following his success at his Primary Examination, but he refused to work for others. He hated the British Raj in Mauritius and their methods of keeping the Indian descendants in some sort of slavery mode. Instead, he chose to lead a life of a gentleman. I understood from Chacha that my Papa always wore his white dhoti and a black woollen jacket no matter the weather. His brown wooden stick became his trademark and he was frequently known as 'Lakri Mamou' (stick man) by his colleagues.

When the bus journey came to an end, I accepted Chacha's invitation to go to his house where we continued the story. I further learnt from Chacha Motilal that my Papa owned at least five acres of land. Prior to his marriage to my mother, the family comprised five people: Papa, Dadi, Dada, his brother, who was two years younger than him and his youngest sister. My Dada died when Papa was only thirteen years old, when travelling to India on his first visit to his family in Ghazipur, as part of his contract as an indentured labourer.

Papa was only eighteen years old when he married my mother in an arranged marriage. She was only fourteen. As was the custom at that time, the bride and groom only set eyes on each other on their wedding day. The Indian custom had remained alive despite the fact that a whole generation had spent their lives in Mauritius as indentured labourers of the British.

I doubt my parents had anything in common. My mother was brought up in a rich economic environment by her Chacha. They had many acres of fertile land in the hills of Vallée des Prêtres. Although my mum had become an orphan at the age of ten, she and her older brother and younger sister were all well looked after by her Chacha. She had everything any girl could want, except the opportunity for formal education, which was a taboo subject for girls at that time. My mother was therefore illiterate when she married my father, but she was a very bright person with a forceful personality. She was only five feet and one inch tall with dark skin, but she always looked straight into your eyes when she spoke.

Ma's illiteracy did not add much spice to their relationship. While my Papa could read and write English, French and Hindi, Ma could not share these delights. The refusal of my Papa to work for others did not help their situation either. Living as a gentleman and as a landlord of only five acres of land which were bought by my Dada with his hard-earned money, soon led to many economic problems. Even when they started feeling the pinch of poverty my Papa refused to work for others, particularly the British. Chacha

Motilal reiterated that Papa was totally against the British rule in Mauritius. The British had defeated the French and taken control the Island of the Dodo in 1810, and administered it as one of her English counties. He felt Mauritians were slaves of the British and to work for them only meant increasing their wealth and power.

According to a village elder, my Papa's daily routine was to get dressed in his white dhoti, take his cane and stroll to his land to oversee his workmen. With the help of Dadi and Ma, he would plant sugarcane, sweet corn and peanuts. The produce was sent to the Port Louis market where it was sold by a middleman, who naturally took a big cut from the profits. Soon, in order to maintain his standard of living, my Papa started mortgaging and selling the land. According to Chacha Motilal, he then became depressed and began befriending ganja pushers.

'I am positive, Jaysingh, that the village ganja pushers deliberately targeted him. He was the only educated man in the village, and he belonged to the upper Hindu caste. Since your Papa always behaved in a superior way, some of the lower caste villagers did not like him. I think they were determined to destroy his life through ganja addiction.'

By degrees, my Papa became addicted to ganja, and his life revolved around people who were able to maintain his addiction. My Dadi always blamed the ganja pushers for the plight they were thrust into at that time. But I believe it was a combination of many factors that led to the sorry state of their lives. His stubbornness in leading the life a gentleman did not help.

'Hello, Jagdeo bhay. Aaj kaise ho?' (How are you today?) The pushers would taunt, luring him towards more drugs. 'See what I have got for you.'

At first, he could afford to pay for every purchase that he made. But when the addiction took hold, he mortgaged the remainder of the land. Later, without any remorse or any thought for his family, he even started stealing money from Dadi and Ma to sustain his addiction.

'I am sorry to say, Jaysingh, said Chacha Motilal, 'that it was a blessing in disguise that your Papa died quickly, as he was intoxicated with ganja. He fell from the boat in deep water. As he could not swim, it took a while for the lone fisherman to rescue him'.

This was the first time I heard the truth about my Papa's death under the influence of ganja.

Chapter Three

Shortly before my birth, Ma decided to live separately from my Papa. It was very unusual at that time for a Hindu woman to desert her husband and live in the same village while her husband was still alive, but circumstances had forced her hand. Ma could not take any further insults and beatings from my Papa. His ganja addiction had brought their lives to the brink of starvation. The last straw came when he started taking the money she had set aside to buy basic foods and squandered it on ganja. But what saddened me most of all was to learn that this educated man was content for his wife to collect fodder for the cow and goats on her own in the blazing sun.

My Papa seemed oblivious to the dire state of his family. When the income from the land dried up, he started using the milk money and even Dadi's pension to furnish his addiction. And besides wasting Ma's savings, he often used the milk that was the sole source of our income to batter ganja with his 'bad friends', as my Dadi called them. Therefore, two weeks prior to my birth, my mother stormed out of the family house despite Papa's protest that he was still the man of the house and Ma, being his wife, must obey his orders. When he, at last, realised the seriousness of his situation, he pleaded with Ma that he would never repeat such evil things. Ma refused to listen to his excuses.

'It is too late now,' she said.

She had been in such a situation many times before. Ignoring him, my mother took her animals, her three children, Didi, Hemsingh and Janee, and walked out on him to a rented accommodation two roads away. My Dadi equally disgusted with my Papa's behaviour, decided to leave as well, to the great consternation of the neighbours and in particular her two sisters who lived nearby.

'You are a disgrace to your family,' Dadi told him. 'This is the only way you can learn. Unless you transform your habits of ganja smoking, we shall never live with you again.'

'Please, don't leave me behind,' Papa pleaded yet again. 'I cannot help myself. I'm ashamed of myself and hate the plight of my family. You must try to understand, the village ganja pushers have made me what I am today.'

'Then you're a weakling. I'm giving you three months to better yourself. Otherwise, you are to spend the rest of your life fending for yourself. I shall pray for you.'

With these warning shots they left my Papa behind on his own, hoping that he would learn from his mistakes. Our Blakie, the ever faithful and agreeable dog of the family, looked at my Papa with her piercing eyes, glanced around several times and grudgingly trod in Dadi's path with her tail tightly tucked between her legs.

The new accommodation had belonged to a friend of my mother's whose husband was in prison for assaulting a neighbour in a land dispute. As he was locked away for a year, the lady was grateful to receive ten rupees a month for a leaking hut that was only used by her two goats. This sugarcane thatched house had just two rooms. It had a hard floor, which was plastered with cow dung. It was surrounded by a two-meter stone wall and the roof was supported by raffia poles. In one of the rooms Ma kept her animals, the other the family used for sleeping and cooking.

Our relatives, and the majority of the villagers, never forgave Ma for leaving our Papa, although the separation lasted only six months. Dadi's two sisters and our cousins stopped coming to see us. The sisters even spread false rumours in the village according to my Dadi

'Have you heard the news, Sabit?' a tall woman, wrapped in a torn, red sari, asked, slowly tilting her head towards Saroja.

'What news, Didi?'

'Indranee has left her husband'.

'No!'

'Yes, she has a lover in the next village. I have seen them together,' the tall woman replied with a sneering look.

'Stop this nonsense you two,' Saroja intervened with glaring eyes. 'Indranee deserves to be free from the abuse and violence she suffered at the hands of her husband. This stupid rumour must stop. It is cruel to say she has another man.'

But the rumour never stopped. Our family was ousted by the village Elders who sided with my Papa. One or two of the ganja pushers exploited the situation further and started meeting with my Papa at our previous house to enjoy their ganja. According to Chacha Motilal, my family's humiliation was unbearable at that time. Chacha persuaded Dadi and Ma to return to my Papa and get rid of the ganja pushers.

Ma was a tough woman. She did not care what the villagers thought of her. But, in the end, the whole family had to return, because she could not afford to continue paying the rent.

My Papa did not see me while we were living in the rented accommodation. Neither Dadi nor Ma made any effort to tempt him there. Ma was determined to teach him a lasting lesson. She thought that depriving him of the sight of his second son was in itself a great punishment.

'He tried to kidnap you, Jaysingh,' Dadi once told me, with her usual toothless grin. 'On that morning your Ma was away in the field as was her routine, cutting grass for the animals. I was alone with you. I had left you on the floor while I was making my tea. When I returned, I saw the outline of a white figure crouching over you. With my failing sight, I thought I had seen a ghost and started shouting 'Bhoot, bhoot.' The neighbours came running and saw a friend of your Papa holding you in his arms and carrying you away.'

It was comforting to know that despite his misdemeanours my Papa did love me. It is a shame I have no recollection of him playing with me.

Chapter Four

It took a while for my family to come to terms with life without our Papa. Some of the neighbours, who were mostly from a lower caste, were very supportive. At least once a day one or two women were in the house helping Dadi with the domestic chores.

Although we were poor in material terms, we never starved. The milking cow was our main source of our income. As well as providing us with milk, we were able to make ghee and sour milk, which we mixed with sugarcane juice and drank with great relish. When the cow went dry, we had an income from the work Ma did in the sugarcane fields for the white farmers. For ten hours work, she received two rupees. After six days work, Ma had barely enough money to buy essentials like flour, potatoes and rice. We rarely bought bread from the shop or the bread merchant; as such luxury was beyond our means. The bread merchant visited the village every morning. We could hear the sound of his bicycle's bell and the voices of the village women and children purchasing his bread. Some mornings I would run to the bread merchant, not to buy any bread but just to see the sight of those crusty rolls. On very special occasions, Ma would give me enough cents to buy one roll. My siblings and I would divide the roll into equal parts and, accompanied by curry, devour it with great satisfaction. Nearly every morning my older sister made roti for us. Although the warm roti tasted really nice, I still craved the merchant's bread and was caned quite frequently for asking Dadi for some cents to buy a roll.

The whole responsibility of ensuring the health and wellbeing of the family rested on the shoulders of Ma and Dadi I never recalled having any sort of toys in the house or any books. Until I was five years old, my constant companion was my Dadi. She would take me everywhere. I hardly saw my mother during this period of my life, as she spent most of her daylight hours either cutting grass for the animals or working in the sugarcane fields.

In a way, we were very lucky to have our Dadi still alive. Her monthly pension of ten rupees partly relieved our economic plight at that time. Despite my tender age of six years, I remember the moments when my siblings and I would wait with great anticipation for the momentous day when she collected her pension. I was the only one who was allowed to accompany Dadi on her walk to the local post office, about half a mile away, following the morning prayer to our most revered God, Hanumanji. Although she was partially blind as a result of her long-standing diabetes, she would support herself with her right hand on her walking stick and her left arm over my shoulder. We trod along the muddy road, bare foot of course, be it rain or sunshine. I remember Dadi always bowed in front of the white officers, when they handed over to her the ten rupees in shiny coins, nearly touching their feet.

On the way home, we would pass by a mansion that belonged to a very rich Hindu landlord. The two-storey house was built using white bricks. It must have had more than ten rooms. There was even a car on the drive, a red Citroen. In front of the house was a long rectangular pond full of sparkling, crystal clear water. I was mesmerised by the fountain which spurted water out of the pond at least four metres into the air. We sometimes saw a boy in the garden. He was similar in age to me and was often dressed in a cream-coloured Nehru suit, an outfit that was very unfamiliar to me. At times, I saw him sitting on a well-padded swing, being pushed by his Dadi. They would laugh and the boy would often yell 'higher, higher'.

We would stand spellbound for several minutes in front of the metal gate in our ragged clothes peering through the gaps between the metal bars, gazing at the architecture of the house, its whitewashed walls, the dazzling fountain and the beautiful red roses that grew around the pool.

Those roses fascinated Dadi and one day she plucked up enough courage to ask the gardener whether she could have a flower.

'No Dadi, Master will punish me if I do that. You can buy one though. Every Friday we cut them and send them to the city to be sold. I suppose only rich people can afford to buy them.'

But the gardener was kind enough to occasionally let Dadi smell a red rose. This celebratory sniffing was always done at the side of the house where the master could not see us. I can still visualise Dadi daintily sniffing at a bloom. She never rushed when the gardener presented one to her. Although she was not allowed to touch the flower, she held the gardener's hand tightly, took a deep breath, brought her wrinkled nose to the rose, and then scanned it from every angle.

I was more fascinated by the sight of the boy: his shiny black leather shoes, the metal swing and his laughter. He would glance at us, not with any malice, but as entertaining objects.

'Dadi'

'Yes, beta.'

I did not know how to say it. I hesitated for few minutes and sighed several times.

'Why are we so poor, Dadi? I want to live like that boy. He has so many beautiful things, and I have nothing.'

With pleading eyes, I would ask the same question every time we passed that big house.

'We are not poor, beta,' Dadi would always answer. 'As long as you are healthy you can never say you are poor. One day you will become like them, if you are prepared to work hard for it. Life is like the rising and setting sun. When the sun shines, it sometimes casts shadows on other objects. But, as it revolves over the sky, very often the shadowed objects get their chance to be bathed in the glory of the sun's light. So, you should never worry over such things. We are in shadows now; there will come a time when those rays from the sun will shine on our fortunes.'

Although I understood some aspects of what she was trying to impart to me I still felt very sad at the thought that Hanumanji did not like us. I resolved to concentrate more on my praying habits; I would clasp my hands firmly together in front of my forehead and chant the mantra clearly every morning, so that fortune would one day smile upon us and I too would have a metal swing like that little boy and wear shiny shoes.

Family misery and envious thoughts were soon forgotten when Dadi bought the juicy, red sweets from the village corner shop of Mr Wang. At such moments, I thought I was the richest boy in the whole village. Unfortunately, I was not allowed to eat any of the sweets until we arrived safely home and my siblings had their share. I remember being very cross with Dadi on several occasions for sharing the sweets equally with my sisters, my brother and my friend Bhardoj. After all, I thought, I was the one who bought them. Sadly, this monthly ritual came to an end when I reached the age of seven years, as Dadi had become totally blind. The task of bringing the monthly pension was allocated to my brother, who refused to take me with him. He thought it was not cool to be accompanied by a younger brother. He preferred to go to the post office with several boys of his own age. From then on I never received any sweets. I missed the journey to the post office but most importantly the sight of the big house and the rich boy, his smile and his friendly gesture towards me.

Chapter Five

Our Dadi was the pillar of the family. She was the eldest daughter of an indentured labourer who came from Bihar, India. At the time of her birth, Mauritius was a British colony. The British defeated the French and conquered the Island of the Dodo in 1810. In order to ensure the supply of sugar to Great Britain was maintained to satisfy the taste buds of the upper and middle classes, the British brought indentured Indian labourers en masse to plant sugarcane. Between 1842 and 1882, about 232,802 migrants came to the island. As slavery was already abolished by the Slavery Abolition Act of 1833, the British colonies were in a dire state owing to a shortage of manpower. By inventing the unique system of indentured labour, the sugar estate companies of Mauritius were able to maintain a constant flow of Indian labourers in the field.

The indentured labourers were poor recruits from Bihar, Punjab, and Calcutta. My Dada was four years old when he arrived in Mauritius. According to my Dadi Dada was an orphan. A distant relative took pity on him and brought Dada with him to Mauritius in 1878. His Immigration Ticket shows that he came from Ghazipur, a town in the state of Uttar Pradesh. According to the protocol of that time my Dada's Immigrant Ticket number was 385236. Most of the recruits were unemployed men and women, and some even beggars. The majority had no idea of the location of Mauritius, with some thinking they were to be transported by ship to another part of India.

Initially, the indentured workers came on a five-year contract. On their arrival they were each sent to a sugar plantation. My Dadi, who was born in 1878, grew up on one of the sugar estates in the district of Rivière du Rempart.

Before the arrival of such indentured labourers, the sugar plantations were manned by French African slaves. At first the Indian migrants were mere experimental 'free labourers', as the sugar companies were emerging from slavery. These companies had little experience of cash crop agriculture. Accordingly, the indentured labourers were treated like slaves. They had to work from seven in the morning till six in the evening with a two-hour break at lunch under the supervision of free African slaves. If allocated work was not completed on time, they were severely punished: their pay was deducted and food ration curtailed. They lived in groups on the sugar estates in thatched huts that had muddy floors and no sanitation. At the end of their contract, the labourers had a choice either to return to their homeland or live outside the sugar estates. It was part of their contract that the return passage was to be paid by their landlords. Therefore, if an indentured labourer decided to stay on at the termination of his contract, their French landlord helped them to buy land and provided them with the amount of cash it would have cost to pay for a sea passage to India.

At the end of their contract, my Dadi*'s* parents and my Dada decided to stay in Mauritius. Following their arranged marriage, they had three children: two boys and a girl. My Papa was the older son, and was born in the year 1907. Despite having three young children, my Dada became restless and booked a passage in 1920 to visit India and see some of his cousins. On the journey he contacted an infectious disease and died on board the ship. My Dadi remained a widow until her death. She supported her three children by working in the sugarcane fields as a labourer of the French landlords.

Dadi was a great storyteller. Every night we siblings sat and slept by her. I occupied the prime position: sitting on her lap, gazing at her in anticipation as she prepared herself for the task. Each one of us had a favourite story, and every time we jostled and begged Dadi to tell our favourite story first. Since we never agreed, Dadi would always end up telling the same stories every night in order to please each one of us. She would rotate the sequence of her narration, so we more or less knew whose story would be told first on any particular evening.

I always slept on her right outstretched hand, while my sisters and brother would fight among themselves to sleep on her left hand. This meant that our poor Dadi always tended to sleep flat on her back. Every morning around four, amidst the sounds of birds, cockerels and barking dogs, Dadi would wake us up singing in a low voice:

Awake; awake my beautiful boys and girls, my golden children.
The sun is shining, the cockerels are crowing, the dogs are barking.

Awake; awake my precious children, my sunshine.
It's time to open your eyes and be grateful to the world you are living in.

Be gracious to your mum, be gracious to your neighbours,
Walk tall, walk high, oh my golden children.

Learn to count and learn to read;
They will be your saviours.

As I translate the song from Hindi to English, it does not sound the same. Somehow the English words do not create the atmosphere of those days. Memories gush in, with alternating bouts of sadness and elation, as I visualise Dadi lying on the bed in a supine position with both hands outstretched, then hugging us and kissing us in turn: always three times on each cheek and forehead. Oh, those happy days. Why did they have to end?

On one such evening, I insisted that Dadi should tell the story of my birth. I said I did not want to hear anymore the stories of Indian Kings' children, but my own. My three siblings hushed at the suggestion, and all agreed as long as they could each have their birth story told.

'Well, we all have to sit up,' said Dadi 'Bring the wooden plank.'

My brother ran to the yard and brought the plank. Dadi sat upright, the plank acting as a cushion for her back, and dug deep in her memory.

It was Saturday 29 September 1945. The weather was foul and cyclonic, a foreboding sign to a full-term pregnant mother living in a dilapidated thatched house. I was already two days late in showing myself. My three siblings sat huddled together, clasping tightly the hands and waist of our Dadi and watching chunks of the thatch being blown away from above their heads. Outside flashes of lightning and the rumble of thunder rattled the eucalyptus poles that supported the porous roof of our two-bedroom house. The cow dung floor slowly dissolved into a muddy stream, soaking the multicoloured, tattered sari of Dadi and the feet of my older brother and two older sisters, to whom I had yet to be introduced. Such weather was commonplace. Two weeks previously a similar cyclone had nearly torn our house apart. This time the wind was even stronger, blowing the trees and terrifying my siblings. But my Dadi as usual, kept her cool.

Holding her sari with her left hand, Dadi cast a sad look at the children, took a deep sigh and at last murmured:

'This is a dreadful omen. The cyclone season always starts in February, not in September. I wonder what kind of sibling you are going to have. You must all now pray to our Lord Vishnu, as he is always very generous and often works in a mysterious way. Perhaps this child will bring some luck to us, who knows.'

She sighed again.

'Another mouth to feed,' she said, looking at the sky. 'Hemsingh, behave yourself. Go and see what your Ma is up to. I have told her to rest. The child is due, but she has to fret over those animals.'

Although Ma was on the verge of bringing me into this world, her priority at that time was to ensure that our milking cow, Ramu, and the two goats had enough fodder during her childbirth. So, despite the cyclonic weather, she got up at four in the morning and dragged her swollen body to the sugarcane field belonging to the white farmers to cut the green leaves. She then walked the two miles home carrying the heavy load on her head, nearly dropping me from her womb many times.

Ma never relied on the sacred blessing of one Lord. She had to pray to both Lords to be doubly sure that her entreaties had been heard. I imagine the sound of the howling weather, with its accompanying thunder and lightning, and the incessant sounds of Ma praying to Lord Rama and Lord Vishnu for a fair-skinned son rather than a girl, must have increased my curiosity to see the outside world at last. For it was during this storm that I must have kicked her hard. I have been reminded many times subsequently that I was a very naughty child well before I came to this world.

So, Ma, having ensured that the animals were safe in the adjoining room of the house, and her children were fed on what was left of the sweet corn roti, cooked two days previously, decided it was time for my Dadi to call for the village woman.

‘Ab aurut ko ando neh.’ (Now, you can call the village woman).

At last, the signal my Dadi was hoping for came to her relief. Despite the early hour, it was decided the village woman should be sent for straight away.

In our little village, it was common practice to seek the help of a village woman during childbirth. Such a woman was not a qualified midwife. Her only qualification was that she had given birth to at least four children and was a respected middle-aged person, living in the same village, belonging to the appropriate Hindu caste. At that time qualified midwives were unheard of in the village. The government had established a state midwifery service, but they only operated in the main towns. There was a private hospital, which was fully equipped with key specialties, but such a service was reserved for the whites only. Anyway, I cannot imagine my *Dadi* would have trusted a professional midwife.

My older brother, Hemsingh, who was then five years old, was assigned to the task of fetching the village midwife. According to him, he ran the one mile to convey the tiding of my impending arrival without stopping, bare foot. My brother has proudly reminded me many times that without his gallant effort I would not have been here today. I don’t remember ever thanking him for his manly effort, as from a young age he was always the man of the house.

Had my Papa been around, being a confirmed ganja addict, he would surely have been in a land of his own, thanking the ganja angels for taking him away from the misery that I was due to bring him; for he never stopped cursing Ma for becoming pregnant yet again.

'You've chosen a fine night, Indranee, to disturb me,' the village woman yelled when she stepped onto the muddy floor, while the thunder and lightning continued to rage outside.

'I'm sorry, Parbho. It seems our Ramaji wanted it that way,' Ma replied with her head bowed, giving a quick glance at our Dadi.

'Well, I don't like to be disturbed at such an hour and to please our Ramaji. I'm going to charge you ten rupees.'

'But Parbho, that isn't right. How are we going to pay you such a large sum?' Dadi and Ma pleaded, their hands clasped in front of them as if praying to Lord Ramaji.

The village midwife would have none of it. She knew very well that Dadi and Ma had no other choice. In the end the matter was settled; she would take one of the goats in lieu of her fee. I was clearly pleased that the issue was resolved amicably and quickly and I didn't have to stay in the darkness of the womb any longer. I came to this earth in a rush, with very little help from the village lady, feeling the cow-dung floor through the thin sugarcane leaf mattress.

I was born only a few months after the capitulation of Nazi Germany to the Soviet Union. While the other side of the world was in a celebratory mood, Ma had important things to worry about.

'Why are you so sad, Indranee?' the village woman asked Ma.

‘Oh, nothing,’ Ma replied. ‘I’m only thinking of the cow and the goats. I hope they’re fine. This weather makes them very restless. I’m worried I haven’t left enough fodder for them.’

‘Don’t think of the cow at such a time, Indranee. Think of your newborn. He is a boy. You should feel proud of yourself for giving birth to a second boy rather than a girl.’

How could she not think of the cow? The cow was her family’s redeemer. If anything had ever happened to her *Ramu,* it was guaranteed that our life would have become a misery, as we were one of the poorest families in the village.

How was she going to feed another mouth? Ma turned her head sideways and looked at me for the first time. I do not think that the sight of me was able to lighten her mood.

‘Why is he so black?’ Ma asked Parbho, in great agitation. ‘The others have fair skin.’

‘He isn’t any darker than your cow, Indranee,’ the village woman assured Ma.

‘Well,’ Ma replied with deep sigh, ‘a black boy is after all better than a fair looking girl.’

‘Of course,’ Parbho replied.

Chapter Six

The main religions of Mauritius are Hinduism, Islam, Christianity, Confucianism and Buddhism. I was born into a Hindu family. Hinduism supports the strict social hierarchy of the caste system. My Dada belonged to the Chhetri caste, the 'warriors and rulers', who are believed to possess qualities of heroic mind, resourcefulness, courage and generosity. Members of the Chhetri caste always have a forename ending with the suffix 'singh'.

Our caste was in a minority in the village. The majority of the villagers belonged to the Vaishya castes, who in theory are merchants and farmers. There was also a Muslim household amidst the fifty-five families in our nagri.

In 1945, the year I was born, Mauritius was very much part of the British Empire. It is roughly the size of greater London and is divided into nine districts. Our house stood in Maheshwar Nagri, a small hamlet within the village of Triolet in the district of Pamplemousse in the north-western part of the island.

Most of the houses in the village were made of sugarcane thatch. Nearly all were of similar shape. They comprised two or three rooms and a veranda, with an adjoining cow shed. The floor and the walls were typically plastered with cow dung. Those who were better off even had a purpose-built thatched kitchen that stood some paces away from the house. Nearly all the houses in our nagri were sited along the dusty roads radiating from the crossroads at its centre. Our house was situated near a sugarcane field on the road heading to the north-west. There was no running water or electricity. Until I was nine years old, the only source of water in the village was a well that was situated nearly a mile away. Twice a day, once at five in the morning and then at six in the evening, I remember trooping along the muddy road with my two sisters, barefoot, singing and dancing, each of us carrying a heavy pale of water on our head. We had no indoor toilet, nor a latrine outside. As with every villager, if nature called; we ran outside to the sugarcane fields to relieve ourselves and then wiped our behinds with green leaves or, very carefully, with shiny pebbles. I don't ever remember washing my hands following such an ordeal.

There was much rejoicing and dancing on the day the local council sited a water tap at the crossroads. The fresh water came directly from La Nicolière Reservoir, which is situated in northern Mauritius. The council workers had been busy for months installing the black, shiny metal pipes along the dusty road that connected us to the main Royal Road pipe. On the day when water was connected to the village tap for the first time, all the village Elders were present in their *dhotis*. The sight of sparkling water pouring from the tap was a miracle to us. We were all lined up according to age to touch the water and open and shut the tap as we were shown by the council officers. That day the villagers flocked to the temple to offer special gifts to Hanumanji. We were thankful that the wind of change had come to our village. But some village Elders were against the centralisation of the water system. They genuinely felt that the tap water was polluted, and many husbands pressured their wives to continue to use the well. However, after a few weeks they were mostly ignored by the village women, whose lives had been suddenly transformed. I for one was reluctant to walk to the well when my friends were using water from the tap. Within a few months, peace again settled on the village, and every householder used the tap.

Now we only had to run to the tap in the centre of the crossroads and run back with two watering cans dangling from each hand. This only took me about ten minutes, as long as there was no queue. Unfortunately, my sisters were soon barred from going to the tap. The village boys loitered nearby and whistled at the girls every time one was seen.

'Ooh, she has pretty legs,' they would shout to each other.

My Dadi therefore, prevented my sisters from going to the tap on their own. They were only allowed to go if they were accompanied by either my brother or myself. I could not have protected them; I was a coward. When the boys started shouting, I would leave my sisters behind and run home as fast as I could. On one such occasion I ran home at such a pace I left my pail behind.

'Where are your sisters, beta?' my Dadi enquired, hitting the large stone she used as an armchair with her curled wooden stick.

'The boys frightened me. They are calling me names, Dadi,' I explained.

Dadi called me over with her usual soothing and comforting voice. No sooner was I within her reach than she got hold of my right ear, gave it a sharp twist and reminded me that I was a man of the house. When I returned to the tap, a big commotion awaited me. Didi, the older sister, was hurling abuse at the boys. Although the boys were still calling my sisters names, I knew they were not frightened. I was quite happy to hide behind Didi's long, flowered skirt all the way home.

Nearly all the villagers were either farmers or labourers. A few owned their own land, from a quarter of an acre to ten acres. They planted sugarcane, tobacco, tomatoes, peanuts and sweet corn. The extra vegetables were sent to the Port Louis market via a middleman who owned a big van. The sugarcane was sent by cart to the local sugarcane factory which was situated three miles from our village in Solitude. The sugarcane factory was owned by the French landlord. The farmers were paid according to the weight of their sugarcane and the amount of sugar their cane was expected to produce. During the limited harvest season all the farmers and labourers were fully employed. They would work from four in the morning till late at night, cutting the canes and transporting them to the factory.

There were no secrets in the village. Everyone knew everyone else's affairs. However, since the caste system was adhered to by the Hindus, my siblings and I were never allowed to eat or drink in houses belonging to a different caste. It was taboo, and I was frequently warned about this by my Dadi We could go to their weddings and participate in all the rituals, but Dadi and my mum always declined to sit with them and eat their food because they were seen as inferior. It was natural that adopting such an aloof posture on our part created an atmosphere of great animosity. An element of distrust existed among us, but it was not shown overtly. Superficially, we all seemed to get on in the village. Rows and fracas occurred frequently among the villagers, but they were never so serious that the neighbourly friendship was permanently affected.

Most of the families, including Ma and Dadi were illiterate. As there was no electricity and no radio or television, information could only be gleaned from those few villagers who could read newspapers. Therefore, most afternoons the Elders were seen sitting at the crossroad of the village gossiping about the politics of the day and any unusual happenings in the village. I never saw any youngsters sitting with them. Perhaps it was seen as disrespectful to mix with these Elders as they were held in high regard by all the villagers.

Despite the caste system, the children always played together and went freely to each other houses. Our favourite pastime was playing marbles. Each player had four marbles to start with. Whoever won the toss would start the game by throwing their first marble. Each player would then try to hit it. The one who hit the most marbles would be the winner. On many occasions a fight would erupt if somebody was caught cheating. I was the skinniest of all with very thin legs, and I don't remember ever winning a fight. I do, however, remember one day playing with a neighbouring boy who hit me quite hard because I was winning. In turn, I gave him two or three blows on his chest and head. When he started crying, I ran home and sat by my Dadi pretending that I had done nothing wrong. Minutes later the boy's parents came to our house shouting and cursing me for hitting their son. Although I tried to explain that he was the one who hit me first, I had to accept that I was guilty and was duly punished by Dadi for my unfriendly action.

The villagers, in the main, would work for the white farmers who owned all the land surrounding our village. They were largely French descendants who managed to cling on to their land and their standard of living despite the British being occupiers of the island. Historical records show that when the British defeated the French in 1810, the conquerors were not interested in farming and management of the land. Agreements were reached that the French would carry on maintaining the land in return for peace and stability on the island and a safe passage to India, so that they could continue their lucrative trade as part of the great East India Company. The labourers did everything. They planted the cane, watered it and during the harvest season cut it by hand and loaded it onto trucks and carts to be carried to the sugar factory. On our way to the sugarcane fields, where we regularly cut grass for our cow and goats, we often saw the white farmers overseeing the workers. They were dressed in khaki shorts and shirts, pith helmets, sturdy boots and long brown socks that would reach just below their knees, despite the searing heat of the day. They travelled in their red Citroën Type 23 trucks, driven by one of their Creole employees. These trucks were a fascinating sight for us children, as nobody in our village owned any sort of motor vehicle. If we saw a truck, we would surround it and give it a close inspection. On one such an occasion, I saw an event that has left an indelible mark on my memory.

'Look, the white man is shouting at Chacha Rajesh,' my friend Arjun whispered to us.

Chacha Rajesh was one of the Elders in the village. He was well respected, married with three children. His eldest son, Ram, was the same age as us. On that day Ram was ill and was not in our company.

We just stood there and watched, aghast. Suddenly, the white man removed his pith helmet and hit Chacha Rajesh on his head with such force that he went reeling to the ground, blood pouring from his head. The other labourers, like us, were just helpless onlookers. My friend Chan attempted to run to Chacha Rajesh, but I held his hands tight. I knew that Chan would have received the same treatment.

Yet, despite the white man's cruelty, we saluted them when they passed us in their trucks or cars. We would stand in line at the side of the dusty road, clasp our hands and bow our heads to them as if they were our Gods. Oh, how I hated them. Despite being only eight or nine, I realised there was an unfair distribution of wealth in Mauritius. I thought then that those white landlords were born to be rich. Along with the hate, I also envied them, and often wondered how they lived, what they ate and what kind of beds they slept in.

At that time most white people lived in Curepipe, which is situated in the middle of Mauritius. In that area the climate is mild, and the summers are cooler than those in the north of Mauritius. However, nearly all these people had second homes along the northern beach where we were forbidden to wander. It was their private beach and locals were not allowed to see how they lived. They only employed Creole personnel, who were then mostly Roman Catholics. These Creoles lived in tiny dwellings built near the beach houses. The French landlords also provided them with fishing boats to catch fish. Any fish left over after the landlords had taken what they wanted the Creoles could sell. At that time of my life, I accepted the status quo without any question. The whites were superior beings; we were their slaves.

Chapter Seven

When my Papa passed away most of our land had already been sold; the remaining one and half acres were heavily mortgaged. We were in debt to a village money lender. Ma had to feed four children, all under ten years old, and she was pregnant with a fifth, my youngest sister Deomatee, who was born seven months later.

I cannot imagine how Ma managed to cope with the plight she was in. Dadi was a great support to her. While Ma was away cutting grass or working in the sugarcane fields, Dadi was there to look after us.

The day after my Papa's death, Ma, with tears in her eyes, found solace in the local temple praying to Ramaji for courage and, most importantly, for some dignity in the eyes of the villagers. She had never been a fully-fledged religious person. But in her own way she followed the Hindu belief that God is there to protect us. The pictures of Vishnu, Ganesh, Ram and Sita and, most importantly, the guardian of the house, Hanumanji, all had a place on the cow dung plastered wall of our house.

Besides Dadi's pension, our main saviour at that time was the milking cow, Ramu that had been given to Ma by her Chacha.

'You look after this cow, betee, and your life will be improved,' her chacha had told her.

According to Ma, her chacha was equally devastated at the sight of the poverty that Ma was facing. He must have felt very guilty for listening to one of his brothers and marrying

Ma to the Woogara family when his own daughters were married into well-known rich households.

Being an orphan, Ma was the favourite child of her eldest Chacha to whom the welfare of the three children, her youngest sister and older brother, was assigned by her own father before he died of tuberculosis. Ma had seven chachas and, at the time of her marriage, all of them lived in the mountainous region of Vallée des Prêtres to the north-west of Port Louis. Ma came from the Servansingh family who were very well known at that time and today are known for famous doctors, lawyers and politicians. The family had hundreds of acres of land on which they mainly grew sugarcane and ginger.

Ma had never known poverty. Her family house was made of bricks with many spacious rooms filled with quality furniture. They had all the trappings of a middle-class family of that time. I remember Ma telling me frequently that she was devastated when she saw the sight of the thatched house on her marriage day, with no decent furniture or beds and with no proper cooking and toileting facilities.

'I did not want to stay in Triolet. I wanted to run away. They were so poor. There was nothing in the house, not even a decent cooking pot. The thatched house was leaking. They had no manners. They were so crude and rough. No privacy in the house. Neighbours could come and go as they pleased and they were always gossiping about each other. They lived like peasants,' she would say with a deep frown.

Ma thought the villagers behaved like savages. Their hair was never combed and the clothes they wore were mostly torn and repaired many times. They hardly ever had a bath and all looked so dirty.

As months passed by, Ma could not stand the poverty anymore. Although my Papa was a decent, educated fellow his foolhardy refusal to work for others was beyond her understanding. She begged her chacha to take her away, as she did not know how she could survive in Triolet, where everybody was poor in every aspect. She told him they lived liked animals with no personal etiquette. In her family house she would eat basmati rice, fish and meat frequently. My Papa's family in Triolet, which comprised Dadi, his younger brother and his sister, had never tasted this polished rice at any time in their lives. At one point, Ma refused to eat the thick rationed rice which was purchased at a subsidised rate. In desperation her chacha bought a hundred kilograms of basmati rice and donated it to my Papa as another gift for marrying his adopted daughter. Her chacha begged my Papa to save enough money to buy another bag when his present had been eaten. Alas, my Papa and Dadi never bought another bag because they never managed to save enough money.

Sadly, according to the Hindu custom at that time, Ma had no choice but to adapt to her new environment. If she had deserted her husband, she would have brought shame to Servansingh family. It would have been an affront to the family and damaged their standing in the community. She had to learn tolerance and perseverance as there was no question of marriage breakdown. As a dutiful Hindu wife, she had to find new ways of surviving in that harsh environment. The girl who had never looked after animals before, apart from her pet dogs, was now determined to forego her rich upbringing and pampered life and embrace the new routine of her poverty-stricken existence. As every avenue was blocked for an outlet to a better life, she promised herself in front of Hanumanji that one day she would drag herself out of this low mode of livelihood. Very soon she made friends with two village women, even though they were from a lower caste. The women accompanied Ma to fetch water from the well. They visited her frequently when she was alone at home and showed her how to cook and carry out the domestic chores. They went together to the fields to search for dry wood for cooking. One of the women even loaned her a goat and, when two kids were born, she was allowed to keep one. From then on, the Woogara family started receiving goat's milk. Dadi was very impressed by the diligence of Ma, and always supported her in every project when my Papa refused to back her. Thus, Ma busied herself looking after her cow and goats and giving birth to children nearly every two years.

Following the death of my Papa, both Ma and Dadi had to adjust to a life where there was no man in the house. By the time my younger sister was born there were five children in the house all under the age of ten. Dadi's daughter was already married and her younger son had died in circumstances that were never talked about in our house. There was a rumour floating in the village that my uncle was murdered by one of the villagers, but this was never discussed.

Ma's priority was to ensure that her children were fed and clothed adequately. She started working harder than ever. Now she kept two cows and at least four goats. She also worked full-time in the sugarcane fields for the French landlords. She decided that another way to ensure her children were well fed was to maintain contact with her rich cousins (Mowsees), most of whom lived in Port Louis and nearby towns. I cannot recall precisely, but probably once every two months we would visit one of them. Ma would wash our only clothes the day before. I remember many times sitting naked, sometimes wrapped in blankets, while my white shorts and shirt were being dried. Even my hair had to be cut and deloused. The local barber, who visited the village once every month, would crop my hair so short that it took months to grow again. I protested to Dadi that my friends laughed at my haircut, since it was the fashion at the time to grow one's hair long. But Dadi's only concern was to save money. To her, style and fashion did not feed her grandchildren.

The barber was a Muslim, but a very dear friend of Dadi He would make me sit on a flat stone in front of our thatched house and bend my neck so hard that I could not move it a single inch. My Dadi sat beside him chatting away gossiping of the village life, and there I was bent double at his mercy. I dreaded the moment when he took out his long black cut-throat razor. I was scared in case his old hands would slip and slice into my neck. But he was a gentle man. He always assured me that he would never harm me, and would then give a gasping chuckle. By the time he finished with me I was stiff, but relieved I did not have to go through the deed again for at least another three months.

Having thus ensured that all her five children were ready, and that the cows and goats had enough fodder, Ma marched us in our newly washed clothes to the bus station where we caught the bus to Port Louis. On such occasions Dadi had to stay behind on her own to look after the animals and guard the house. Her favourite meal, which consisted of curried bomri and roti, was prepared by Ma before she left. As there was no fridge in the house, the metal pans were simply left on the floor, which was custom and practice at that time. Dadi was partially blind by this time, and Ma thought that it was not safe for her to cook her own food, as it involved lighting dry wood. Consequently, Dadi would eat the same prepared meal for nearly three days. Bhardoj's Ma was willing to help, but Dadi was a stubborn lady and determined to maintain her independence at any cost.

On one such occasion, I was particularly unhappy leaving my Dadi behind. I started crying and refused to accompany my family. I was determined to stay with Dadi but my brother and sister dragged me along despite my tremendous protest. I thought it was unfair to leave Dadi behind and alone when her eyesight was failing because of her worsening diabetic condition, and decided to play a clever trick. I allowed my mum and siblings to board the bus first and then ran home as fast as I could to Dadi.

Primarily, I didn't like to go because I hated the idea of leaving my Dadi behind. But also I was disgusted at finding myself in the company of those wealthy Mowsees and their children. We had nothing in common. They were very rich compared to us. Ma was very fond of visiting her eldest cousin in Saint Paul, near Curepipe. They lived in a five-bedroom brick house with very large front and back gardens. They had running water, electric lighting, and indoor toilets, which I was scared to use.

It was during such visits to Ma's cousins that I first saw telephones and the way people could converse on the lines. I also saw maids in their houses doing their cooking on a petrol fired cooker. At our house we used logs and small pieces of wood to cook our food. Most of these families had cars on their paved driveways. We were so simple, so naive compared to them. Besides, with no shoes and wearing patched clothes, the sight of their wealth made me feel very inferior and humiliated in their presence. Despite my tender age I was horrified by the extent of our poverty compared to their wealth and their style of living. At times I thought that our chachas enjoyed showing their wealth to us. I thought they were taking special pride in ensuring that there remained a marked difference between us. I hated and also envied them at the same time. Not once do I ever remember playing with the children, although they were the same age as me. I could see them in their rooms, well dressed with glistening shoes on their feet, reading books and doing their homework. But they never said hello to me, or were even encouraged by their parents to play with me. So, such visits were very lonely occasions, and hurtful to my pride and dignity in many ways.

When it was time for us to return home, Ma's cousins would give us rice, vegetables, lentils and clothes, which we had to carry in our hands and on our heads. We were frequently given the cast-off clothes of our cousins. I would love such gifts. They were always practically new, and I was proud to show them to my friends when I got home.

These visits did have one particular positive effect on me. Ma practically transported us to a different planet, where they ate, dressed and talked very differently from us in the village. The sight of the luxurious, material world fired my imagination and ambition no end. I wanted to become like them and live like them. I wanted to have books, read them and display them on long shelves, as I saw in their houses. I wanted to go to school, be educated and a rich man one day. I even wanted to possess a car and live in a brick house with a swimming pool. The visits, in a way, gave me some sort of purpose in life, an objective I knew I had to achieve.

At that time, I had no idea what I had to do to shake off our poverty. Sadness weighed me down frequently and I would rarely walk through the village with any sort of smile on my face. I became a thinker at a very early age, and would sit under the mango tree at the back of our house, scheming and planning my future, wondering what it would be like being an educated and a wealthy man. The sky was the same everywhere and the same sun was shining on all of us; the level of disparity between us tormented me. I wanted a solution so that I could support my family, but did not know how. Dadi's words tortured me:

'The sun will shine on us one day, beta.'

But I carried on praying for even a glimmer of that elusive light.

Chapter Eight

My Dadi was determined that her grandchildren would receive the basic primary education that was optional at that time from the age of five to twelve years old. She strongly believed that one should better oneself through education. Despite many difficulties she had faced in her life, she had ensured that my father had received a good education. He was the first person in the village to pass his sixth standard examination with good grades. Unfortunately, he failed to exploit this achievement for his own benefit or for the benefit of his family. Dadi failed to explain to us why our Papa did not take a government post. I cannot judge whether he was right or wrong in this decision. But I do know we suffered for his stubbornness.

When I reached the age of four, my older brother and two older sisters were already attending the primary school. I was desperate to join them. Government or privately run pre-primary schools did not exist in our village in those days although there were some regulated private institutions in the main towns. One day, while I was helping Ma to wash the dishes with charcoal dust in the backyard, I asked her whether I could go to school with my brother and sister. She told me I was too young to attend primary school, and she needed help at home and in the fields and somebody to look after the animals. I became rather disillusioned, and thought that Ma was deliberately keeping me away from school. I cried and ran away from our house and hid myself in a bush. I only came home because I became very hungry. I learned subsequently that Ma and Dadi had been frantically looking for me everywhere.

'You naughty boy, you must never do that again.'

Ma slapped my tearful face and dragged me to Dadi to explain my actions. I told Dadi that I wanted to go to school like my brother and sister and become an educated man like my rich cousins. I did not want to cut grass anymore.

'I shall have a word with your mum,' Dadi replied, holding both my hands and kissing them. 'You are still very young. They only take pupils from the age of five years old.'

Without my knowledge, Ma had listened to Dadi and had visited the local privately-run school. I was granted permission to start 9th Mile Primary School, despite my age. It was a charity school about a mile away from our house. At the time it was owned and managed by a rich landlord, but later became a government school. My Dadi knew the landlord and I was allowed, for some reason, to attend the school without paying any fees. The roads to the school were lined with sugarcane fields and, according to the weather, were either dusty or very muddy. Every morning prior to going to school my friends and I had to get up at five in the morning. Following a brief breakfast, which usually comprised of curry and rice left over from the previous night, we went to the fields to cut grass and carry the fodder home in our little arms. By the time I returned, probably around half past seven, I was already worn out. I had no time to wash myself properly. I just had time to clean my feet, pick up my broken slate and slate pencil and run all the way barefoot to school without stopping.

It was at times difficult to judge the precise time as we did not have a clock. When the sun was shining, we were very good in working out the time by looking at the tree shadows. But during the rainy season it was a matter of guessing. Ma could tell the time even when the sky was covered with dark clouds. But when I needed her most, she was always in the fields. Some of my friends frequently refused to accompany me, as they felt it was a waste of time going to school. Bhardoj, my best friend, nearly always followed me to the school. Instead of attending the class with me he would leave me by the gate and run away with other children who were playing truant. Bhardoj would always make me promise not to tell his mother.

I often arrived at school just in time to sing God Save the Queen and Rule Britannia while a spectacular British flag was slowly pulled up a long white pole by one of the teachers. After the morning assembly the class teacher would inspect our hands and feet, and nearly always I was sent to the toilet area where I had to clean them.

The lunch break was between midday and one o'clock. Every day I ran home for my lunch. I never, ever carried my food to school. I suppose my mother could not afford to buy a suitable container. It was unusual among the village children to take food to school. So, at lunch break we all ran to our respective houses. However, there were two children from a wealthy family in our class whose lunch was brought every day by a chauffeur driven car in a shiny three-tiered Tiffin tin. The sight of the daily arrival of the Tiffin tins for the rich boy and girl, around ten in the morning, was the envy of all other pupils in our class. These two children were always dressed in clean white clothes and polished black shoes. They spoke slowly and had gentle manners. They sat on the front bench while my seat was just behind them. I wanted to befriend the rich boy, but I was too shy to approach him. One day, I took three ripe mangoes with me that had fallen the previous night in our back garden. Following the singing of *Rule Britannia*, I gingerly approached him and smiled.

'I've brought these for you. I've specially picked them for you only this morning. They are ripe and juicy.'

He looked at the mangoes and then my dirty fingers, still caked with dry mud. He could tell the mangoes were not fresh. They had slimy marks on them, left by the overnight crawling snails and huge black slugs.

'No, thank you,' he replied, giving a disgusted look at the mangoes and me with my dirty bare feet and patched up shorts.

'We have many mango, papaya and lychee trees.'

Of course, I was very disappointed at his rejection of my overture. Although it was obvious I was well below his status, I was determined to win him in other ways.

At lunchtime I would arrive home panting and breathless. Very often I had to make the meal for both myself and Dadi. It was not a difficult activity, as Dadi would have already prepared the ingredients as best as she could. By this time, she was completely blind. But her sense of orientation was amazing. I would sometimes pretend I was somebody else and mimic different noises when approaching her. But she knew exactly where I was and would call out with great joy in her voice.

'Sona (golden boy), I know you are there,' she would say, pointing directly at me with her walking stick.

We ate together. It was always a very sparse meal, mainly roti and tomato chutney with a mug of water. During the meal it was usual to fill her in with the morning activities at school. It was during this time I shared with her the rejection I felt from the rich boy.

'Don't worry, sona,' she said with a deep sigh. 'You concentrate on your education. You show him by your deeds rather than by how you look. He will accept you one day. Even if he does not, remember it does not matter'.

'But I want him to like me Dadi. I can learn a lot from him. If he became my friend, he could invite me to his big house'.

'You are going to be late to school.'

After the meal, I would run back to school for the afternoon session, which started at one o'clock. I was often punished for being late, either in the morning or at lunchtime. When I tried to explain to the teacher the reasons for my lateness, the other children would laugh at me. The punishment for being late was to be caned in front of the class: one cane lash for every five minutes of lateness. The teacher would call me to the front of the class and make me sit on a high stool. I knew what was going to happen next. I prepared myself for the onslaught of the cane by holding out my open palm. It was extremely painful when the cane fell on the extremities of my fingers. Very often I would cry, and that too became a source of great pleasure for the class. And looking back, I feel the teacher also obtained great delight by caning me. I have never understood why that was. Fortunately, the caning stopped when I moved to the fourth standard.

I enjoyed being at school and was determined to do well. Unfortunately, I did not have the required books as we could not afford to buy them. At that time, everyone had to purchase their own schoolbooks. The majority of pupils possessed them, particularly those children of retired army personnel who had fought abroad with the British soldiers and rich landowners. It was an irony that although we had land, we were poorer than the pensioners who had no land. They at least had a regular monthly income, where as we depended very much on the seasonal crops, the milking cow and the meagre state pension of Dadi

I remember the occasion when I found a schoolbook on the side of the road underneath a bunch of sugarcane plants. It was an English book, the same book our teacher had asked us to buy. I was so excited to obtain it that it did not occur to me that it could have been dropped by a pupil in my class. I hid it quickly under my shirt and ran home to tell Dadi of my treasure. Dadi thought I had stolen the book. Like a lawyer, she cross examined me several times to explain how I found it. After five minutes of intensive questioning, she gave a broad smile and hugged me tightly.

'Beta, I accept your innocence. You are very fortunate to find this book. The child who had dropped the book will be missing it. Therefore, it is your duty to return it to the owner.'

To my great disappointment, Dadi made me promise to return the book to the school and hand it to the teacher. Next day, I had no choice but to comply. The teacher asked me similar questions. Later that morning the rightful owner was located. Her name was Sita, the daughter of the richest landowner in our village. She was delighted I had found her book. From that day we became sort of friends and she started talking to me frequently in the afternoon break. Although, I did not understand why, the teacher equally started showing great affinity towards me. She started making a special effort to check my understanding of Mathematics and English. She lent me her spare Mathematics, French and English books. I was proud and excited that at last I had books of my own to take home like the rich pupils. I became teacher's pet: the envy of my classmates. She made me sit on the front bench where only the privileged children sat. The book incident and the consequences that followed definitely boosted my self-confidence, and made me realise the reward of honesty and sincerity.

It was common practice in our school for those children who could afford to pay tuition fees to receive extra lessons from their class teacher after the last period of the day. I was excluded from such extracurricular sessions, as Ma could not afford to pay such fees. These elite children were receiving extra lessons at least three times a week. Hence, most of them were consistently achieving top marks in all the class tests. They were also doing specific homework in Mathematics, English and French languages. While these children were involved in intensive and serious study, I was sent to cut grass and work in the fields. It was difficult to keep up with the schoolwork, no matter how hard I tried in class. No wonder I was always near the bottom of the class, and got caned for not showing an understanding of the arithmetic problems.

One afternoon, two weeks after the book incident, the teacher (whose name I cannot recall), asked me to stay behind. I said I could not stay behind because I had to cut grass for the animals.

'Okay, then ask your Ma whether you could stay behind for some private lessons from me tomorrow.'

I told Ma and Dadi that evening what the teacher had said.

'We are not able to pay her fees, Jaysingh,' Ma responded, with sadness in her eyes.

But Dadi thought it was an excellent idea.

'Tomorrow, you ask the teacher how much it will cost for these extra lessons.'

Next day, when I told the teacher that my mother could not pay her tuition fees, she hugged me.

'Woogara, don't worry. I am going to help you. You do not have to pay me.'

From then on, I too started receiving private lessons. I sat with pride in my heart with those privileged children, as I knew the teacher did not expect any payment from me. During such occasions, she also gave me pieces of chocolate. It was something I only would have dreamed of receiving at home. It was during this time that I formed a bond of friendship with the rich boy. During the morning break he often, to my great delight, sought me out.

Sadly, this privileged treatment terminated when I moved to the next class where I had to face a new teacher.

Chapter Nine

My siblings and I were too young to plough our land and cultivate them in the same way as the grownups. So, after school and at most weekends my brother and I dug the soil with our tiny pioches (draw hoes). Despite our difficulties, we managed to plant peanuts and sweet corn and later tobacco, but had to employ labourers for the work that was impossible for us to perform. It was difficult to employ such labourers on a regular basis, because of the costs involved. As well as working on the land, we had to bring fodder for the animals. Nearly every afternoon after the school, around five o'clock, when the temperature had dropped by a few degrees, my brother and I would walk together to the fields with our pioches on our shoulders. We worked until darkness fell, carrying back, on our heads, any weeds and grass that were suitable for consumption by the cow and goats. During these trying times my brother and I became great friends. We would plan our future lives should we happen to have some money, and dream together of having a grand house with many rooms and a garden full of beautiful flowers.

'What would you like to be when you grow up?' I would ask him quite frequently.

'I don't know,' he would reply, with great hesitation. 'I have to pass my examination. But what chance have we got when we are spending most of our time here in the fields when others at this very time are studying.'

He would always say the same words and always with great sadness in his eyes. It was obvious looking back that he was already a defeated man well before he took any examinations.

'I want to become a school teacher.'

I stressed those words with great relish in my voice.

'I want to study hard and pass all my examinations, and then I'll go to secondary school. You will see. I am going to have a brick house in which all of us are going to live.'

My brother often refused to go to the fields. He was self-conscious and felt ashamed of working as a labourer when his peers were studying at home. Since he was five years older than me, he was attending a fee-paying secondary school in the city of Port Louis at great sacrifice by my mother. Instead of accompanying me to the fields or studying at home, he started roaming about in the centre of the village. He would befriend only those boys who did not go to school. It hurt me to see him whiling away his time with them. On most occasions, it was left to my mum and I to till the soil and sow the seeds. My sisters were not allowed to work on the land, because such employment would have affected their marriage prospects. Most importantly constant exposure to the sun would have darkened their skin. It was alleged that boys would not marry a girl with dark skin. So, my sisters stayed at home and performed all the household chores, which freed Ma to concentrate on outside work, looking after the animals or our land and, quite often, working as a paid labourer for the sugarcane landlords.

Thus, I grew up during my primary school days worrying about the future of the family. I wondered often what would happen to my sisters. How were they going to be married? I was very conscious that we were extremely poor and thought that my sisters might never get married. Such thoughts horrified me and kept me awake at night.

I must have been ten years old when I reached the fifth standard. My new teacher lived locally in Triolet. I noticed early on that he had the habit of ignoring me, but was very keen to help others who were from the same caste as his own. This was the first time I was made acutely aware of the Hindu caste system. I was deeply hurt when I found out that the teacher formed a group of these pupils and was giving private lessons twice a week at his home, to which I was never invited. It was clear that these pupils were miles ahead of me in the class. The teacher was also lending these children books to complete their homework. I lived in the same village as these boys, and when I asked them to show me what they were studying with the teacher they refused. Such overt discrimination hurt my very soul. I felt very disappointed, and hated myself for belonging to an upper Hindu caste. It brought much heartache to the family and at times caused conflicts with our neighbours and my school friends.

'It's not fair, not fair,' I told my Dadi one day, hugging her and crying aloud, 'that I should be punished for not knowing something when I was never taught. The teacher always shows favour to pupils from the lowest caste families.'

I then divulged to her the state of play within the school, how I felt disadvantaged and how unhappy I was. I told Dadi

I did not want to go to school as I felt humiliated and ignored in the class.

'I want to work in the fields. I can plant sugarcane and earn some money,' I cried.

My Dadi held my wrists with her hard, wrinkled hands, and invited me to sit down by her on the polished stone that we used as furniture on the dusty veranda.

'You won't get education by working in the fields, my boy. If you want to become somebody, you must compete with the very people you feel are hurting you. You should find ways of befriending those pupils who the teacher is helping, and try to learn from them so that you can stay abreast with your study. Education is the passport to success. It is the key to your bright future. Be patient and show determination.'

I listened to her intently and wondered how I was going to improve myself. Although I was a shy boy, with very limited knowledge of the outside world, I was not averse to making friends with the boys from the lower caste. Sundir was my closest friend during this time of my life. We were like brothers. I knew very well that he was receiving special help from another teacher in another village. I often saw him going to these private lessons, particularly in the evenings. One day I managed to persuade him to pretend to the teacher that I was his cousin, and to ask the teacher to help me. Sundir duly took me to an evening session and vowed to the teacher that I was his cousin. On the ride of such lies, I received free lessons for two weeks. Unfortunately, somebody blew the whistle, although I never discovered who. On the third week I was called aside and asked to leave. No explanation was given. I remember returning home crying my heart out all the way. I did not share such a humiliating experience with anybody, not even my Dadi. Such treatment from the teacher made me more determined than ever to show these people that I was equal to them, despite all the disadvantages I was facing.

When I reached the sixth standard, the final year of our primary education, I knew I had to do well. If I could obtain a good pass, there was an excellent chance of obtaining a scholarship and receiving free secondary education in an elite government school. It was the dream of every sixth standard pupil.

I was nearing eleven years old, but underweight compared with the other children in my village, with thin legs like bamboos. Despite this, I was quite good at sports. In the sport sessions I participated in running, jumping in sacks and racing with an egg on a spoon. However, the sport I enjoyed most was playing football. I would play centre forward at the school games and soon became quite prolific in scoring goals. The only snag was I had to play barefoot, as I could not afford to buy any kind of shoes at that time. In fact, I do not remember having any sort of shoes until I was perhaps thirteen or fourteen years old. I did have plastic flip-flops, but they were worn only during visits to our posh relatives in Port Louis or going to weddings.

At school we would play football matches with the other school in Triolet. I remember the occasion when I was selected to play for the sixth standard class on a sports day to which all parents were invited. We were specifically told that every player must wear appropriate shoes. Otherwise, he would be barred from playing. Despite begging Dadi to buy me a pair of pumps, the match day was fast approaching and I was still shoeless. I told the self-elected captain my state of affairs. I knew he was the son of a very rich landlord, since every day his lunches were brought by car. He knew I was very poor, but was always kind to me after I brought him the mangoes. Perhaps, he was impressed by my ability to run fast and score goals. Two days before the vital match, he called me to him during an interval between lessons and told me to wait for him at the end of the school day. To my great surprise and excitement, he handed me a pair of blue linen pumps.

'They're yours, Jaysingh. I persuaded my father to buy this pair for you. Now you can play in the match.'

Despite the initial excitement, I soon realised I was useless as a player when I had the shoes on. Since there were only two days left, I did not have enough time to get used to them. On the day of the match my play as a footballer was abominable. I just could not hit the ball. I still remember we lost 5–0. It was a sad day in many respects. After the match, the rich captain was so upset he confiscated the shoes I thought were mine.

'Shoes are no good for you Jaysingh. You are better off playing with bare feet.'

I sobbed on my way home, not just about losing the match and letting my friends and the class down, but above all about losing the dream shoes. I started hating rich people for the way they were dressed, for everything they stood for. I hated my rich relatives, because I knew that in their presence my personal state stood out. I started feeling inferior in front of these people. I could not share my inner feelings with anybody. While I was in the sixth standard dear Dadi was frequently very ill and febrile because of her worsening diabetes. I did not want to worry her with my problems.

In November 1956 I took my primary school examination with the great hope of success in obtaining a scholarship and entering the Government sponsored school. This would mean that my mother would not have to pay any school fees. On the morning of the examination, I got up at four o'clock. I quickly had a shower with a pail of water. Without anything in my belly, I ran to the temple to pray to Hanumanji for success. Culture dictated then and now that praying with a full belly means showing disrespect to the gods. My Dadi had hammered into me that great sacrifices are required if ever one wanted anything in life, including eating nothing prior to praying.

When I reached the school, I noticed all the lower caste boys and girls were grouped together. I was curious to know what was going on. I had no idea when I approached the group that our sixth standard teacher was standing in the middle and telling them something in a 'hush hush' voice. I knew he was giving the boys inside information, and I wanted to be part of the group and learn anything that could help me in the examination. Some of the boys turned around and gave me a disdainful look. Although deeply hurt by the rejection, I did not lose confidence. I knew Hanumanji would help me, since the lower castes did not believe in His Lordship. I thought I was also fairly well prepared, as for three days I had been revising as best as I could.

'You should stay at home Jaysingh, and revise for your exam,' Ma had said when I got up at the usual time of five in the morning three days prior to the examination.

So, for three days and nights I was freed from going into the fields and cutting fodder for the cow and goats and ploughing the land. Although I felt bored at times, I did feel fresh on the day of the examination. The examination went quite smoothly. I thought I did fairly well in all the subjects: English Language, English Geography, French, Hindi, Arithmetic and Penmanship. Following the examination, life returned to its routine, ploughing the fields as best as I could, cutting fodder for the animals and playing games with the local boys.

Chapter Ten

There are many incidents during my primary school days that I would dearly like to forget, because they bring me so much pain. But there are certain events which are so memorable that it is worthwhile placing them on record.

I must have been eight years old and was lying on the hard bed listless and barely conscious of my surroundings. Our chacha from next-door, who was visiting me frequently, told Dadi I had dysentery and was gravely ill. I could not retain anything in my stomach and had a high temperature and was shivering. Chacha told Dadi I must be taken to the hospital immediately otherwise they were going to lose me. One of the girls in the village had recently died from it, he reminded her forcefully many times.

Dysentery and polio were common in our village. Most of the villagers did not have a latrine, and the physiology of cross infection was poorly understood by them. In our house, as far as I can remember, hand washing with soap and water was unheard of.

Ma and Dadi were very concerned about my health. They kept me cool as best as they could by placing cold compresses on my forehead. Although I could not retain any food, they kept encouraging me to eat something. Every time a neighbour came to see me, Dadi started crying quite loudly. Each neighbour had his own solution for my cure, and every type of herbal medicine was tried on me. My brother was very busy galloping around the fields to fetch plants that had medicinal constituents in them. Still my condition did not improve. I remained very weak in bed for nearly three weeks and had lost a lot of weight.

Dadi was reluctant to send me to the hospital. She did not trust a doctor's medicine to cure me. The only hospital near to our house was in Port Louis. Although by the 1960s Mauritius had started decentralising the health service by building health centres in each district, they were poorly staffed. Even so, all health care in the public sector was free at the point of delivery, and our local Health Care Centre was only half a mile away from where we lived, yet I was not even taken for any form of consultation.

Dadi had already had a bad experience with my sister Didi, who had died of liver failure the year before. She was taken to the Port Louis hospital, but she was sent home by the medical team who thought she would be better off being cared for at home. The prescribed medicine did not work. Dadi always blamed the hospital for her death. In later years, when I did research into her death, I found out that Didi had become addicted to glue. Dadi's ignorance of the actual causal factor of Didi's death nearly killed me too.

One day my Dadi's sister visited me, even though she was not welcome in our house. Ma did not like her, because her husband practised voodoo. It was widely believed in the village that he was a witch doctor, and we were prohibited from going to their house in case he cast a bad spell on us.

'Jaysingh is going to die. Why don't you try the medicine of my husband? In no time he will be cured.'

'Does he want a goat or a hen for his sacrifice?' asked Dadi 'Because at present we cannot afford either.'

'The bigger the animal the more effective will be his spell. You know that.'

Dadi took a deep breath. She looked at me with her forlorn eyes and gave a nod to Ma who was sitting a few metres away. It was apparent that my Dadi's sister had managed to persuade Dadi her voodoo husband would cure me instantly.

Voodoo was widely practised in the village. When somebody was taken ill their first point of call was to the witch doctor rather than a medical practitioner. They only charged a nominal fee and the cost of a sacrificed animal, be it a goat or a hen. It was believed that the practice only worked if the sacrificed animal was eaten by the witch doctor.

One morning, in a semi-comatose stage, I saw a man jumping about around me with both hands raised, calling upon the spirit of his forefathers to remove any bad spells from me. His white dhoti was swinging around him. In one of his hands, he was holding a headless chicken, dripping blood all over me. I was so scared I started screaming. My voodoo chacha reassured my family that the spell was working as I had started shouting, which meant my body was being cleansed. Looking back, I have difficulty in comprehending the extent to which my family placed trust in the healing power of the voodoo chacha, when it was made obvious by our next door chacha that I was suffering from a condition requiring urgent medical help. Despite the voodoo treatment, my condition worsened for another few days. Dadi became convinced nothing was going to cure me.

Next, the Hindu pundit was called. He gave me last rites and said my soul would leave my body in two days' time. While performing his mantra he placed a red *tika* on my forehead and under my chin. The pundit advised Dadi that every evening until my death a vigil should be held and certain mantras should be sung by my bed. However, instead of dying I started recovering. According to Dadi and Ma, it was a miracle I survived.

Following my recuperation, the pundit was brought back and a lengthy puja was held to thank the various gods who were thought to have helped my recovery. All our close relatives were invited except the voodoo chacha and chachee.

As well as voodoo doctors, palm readers were very popular in the village. As the majority of the villagers were very poor, they wanted to know if some good fortune was awaiting them. There was a very old lady in the village. She must have been ninety years old. It was alleged that she could tell anybody's future – at a price of course. One day, it must have been a few weeks after my miraculous recovery from dysentery, Dadi asked me to accompany her to that old, wrinkled lady.

'Dadi, I do not want to go. She is frightening. Every time I see her, she glares at me.'

'Don't worry. I shall be with you. I want to know what your future holds for you. God has saved you from the ultimate death. His Lordship must have thought you have a lot to contribute. Let us go and see what the old lady says life has in store for you.'

I was more or less dragged there. Most of my friends thought she was a wicked witch. But, to my surprise, she was very welcoming. She had pleasant manners and asked us to sit on the cow dung floor as there were no chairs in the house. We were offered tea in special china mugs, not tin mugs as we had in our house. When I finished my tea, she asked me to make three circles around my head with my empty mug and place it in front of her. She leaned forward and peered at the empty mug and shouted with great elation.

'Aha Didi. Jaysingh has a great future. These leaves show he is going to travel abroad. Hold on, your beta is going to be a rich man, too. Oh, what a future he has. You see there is a reason why our God has saved him. I think he is going to do some good things in the future.'

'But I don't want him to travel abroad, Didi. You know what happened to my husband. Surely, he can still be a rich man without travelling abroad.'

'I am only telling you what I can find here. You should be delighted as his future is very bright indeed.'

Dadi was not very pleased when we left the old lady's house.

'Jaysingh, you have to promise me that you will never ever travel abroad.'

'I promise, Dadi, I will never leave you behind to travel to another country.'

There are other memories I still treasure from my time as a primary school pupil. It was not all doom and gloom. Not only did I enjoy participating in school sports, I also enjoyed studying for my examinations. Although examinations can generate great stress, they were important to me because they were the only means to show how I was performing in my school subjects. Dadi and Ma being illiterate and my brother indifferent about my progress, there was nobody at home who could progressively monitor my performance in my school subjects.

The school frequently organised trips to visit various places in Mauritius, but I do not remember ever going on any of them. They had to be paid for by the parents, and sadly I was always left behind while my school friends were able to enjoy themselves and expand their knowledge and experience.

One morning, when I was in the sixth standard, our teacher informed us that, as Princess Margaret, the Countess of Snowdon, was visiting Mauritius, all children from the fifth and sixth standards were invited to celebrate the occasion and provide the warmest welcome. The important news to me was that the school would pay for the trip, but we were required to wear clean white shirts, shorts, shoes and white socks and bring our own luncheon. It was stressed that flip-flops should not be worn as it was a special occasion. The trip was planned for the 1 October 1956, and we were all to travel to the Pamplemousse Botanical Garden by bus.

It was one of my happiest days at school. I ran home to give Dadi the great news.

'Are you sure, Jaysingh, the teacher said that the trip will be paid by the school?'

'Yes Dadi.' I was jumping up and down in great excitement as it was going to be my first ever trip with my school friends.

'What else did the teacher say?' she queried, in her usual calm voice, looking straight into my eyes to check that I was being truthful.

'Nothing in particular Dadi, except that we have to wear clean white shirt, shorts, shoes and white socks. He said flip-flops will not be allowed.'

'We have to tell your Ma to buy you a new shirt, trouser and a pair of plimsolls. Did you say a pair of white socks too? I have some money saved from my pension. Perhaps that would help.'

'Yes Dadi, some of my friends are having leather shoes. Can I have leather shoes instead of plimsolls?' I said those words with great excitement.

I waited for Ma's arrival from the fields with great trepidation, as Dadi's words had reminded me of our financial plight. By the time I mentioned to Ma about the trip I knew the answer already.

'But Ma, please, I have never been on any school trips. This trip is being paid for by the school. I think all the school children from our class are going. I want to see the Queen.'

We all thought Princess Margaret was the Queen. I had no idea of the difference between a princess and a queen.

Ma was adamant that she could not afford to buy new shirt, shorts and a pair of shoes. But she would definitely find a way for me to go on the trip. I hugged Ma so fiercely that we nearly fell down on the ground, and ran to Dadi to give the great news.

Although the Primary School Examination was due to take place in November of that year, the main topic of conversation among my friends was the forthcoming trip to the Pamplemousse Botanic Garden to see Princess Margaret. At school we had a special period when everything about Britain was taught, particularly the greatness of the kings and queens of England and the importance of the mother country in the world. The teacher had reminded us that it was a once in a lifetime occasion to see a princess of England.

Some of my friends had already been to the tailor to have their special uniforms measured for the trip. At least four of them were going to have new leather shoes. At that time, I did not even possess a pair of plimsolls. I really envied my friends who were talking of having a pair of leather shoes.

'What are you going to wear, Jaysingh?'

'New clothes and black leather shoes, I think,' I said with great excitement.

Despite my incessant pleading for a new uniform for the trip, sadly, it never materialised. I shall never forget my disappointment and sadness on that day. At first, I refused to go to the school trip in my old patched shorts and shirt. I was told to wear my brother's flip-flops. Since the flip-flops were too big for me, Ma tied them with a piece of her old white sari around my ankles.

'You look great, my sona,' Ma said. 'Off you go or the bus will leave without you.'

I told Dadi the children would laugh at me and the teacher had specially told us to wear shoes and socks.

'There is nothing to be ashamed about, sona. The teacher will understand.'

I did not realise Ma had already been to see the teacher, who lived in another village, to plead my case. So, when I arrived at school with my luncheon in a small sack, I was surprised to receive pleasant greetings from all my friends and the teacher. Some of my friends even hugged me. Nobody questioned the state of my clothing or my shoes or the fact that I was not wearing a pair of white socks. I was puzzled, for everybody was so friendly towards me. It was later that I found out that the teacher had warned all the students not mention the state of my attire.

We arrived at our destination singing, in a jolly mood and waving our British flags from the bus windows. On our arrival, we joined a huge crowd of children from different schools. We all lined up by the main house, situated in the middle garden where the princess, as tradition demanded, was due to plant a commemorative tree. We were told to wave the flags vigorously the moment we saw the princess. I wanted to be in the front row with my friends, but the teacher advised me to stand next to him in the third row. I did not mind, and felt very privileged to hold a position next to our teacher.

Around eleven o'clock there was a great commotion in the crowd. We saw Princess Margaret arriving in a jeep. She was standing and waving at the crowd. She was wearing elbow length white gloves, a tiny hat, black, high-heeled shoes and a beautiful white floral dress. She was flanked by tall white men in white uniforms, one of them Sir Robert Scott, Governor of Mauritius. We all surged forward en masse, and started waving our flags as we were taught to do. It was an amazing occasion that I shall never forget. Here was a British princess who we had read about in our history books, standing in front of us, holding a shovel and planting a small tree.

'Well, did you see the Queen?' Dadi asked; when I reached home around four o'clock.

'No Dadi we saw Princess Margaret. She is the sister of the Queen.'

'Where did you eat your food?'

'We all sat in circles to eat our food, by a lily pond.'

I did not mention to Dadi that my friends had brought their food in shiny aluminium containers wrapped in a clean cloth. They were eating curry and rice instead of one dried roti with onion salad, as I was. In my excitement I nearly let the cat out of the bag about sharing the curry and rice of my friend, Doshee, who belonged to a lower caste. I often wondered what kind of punishment I would have received, had I divulged my indiscretion in crossing the caste boundary. But Doshee and I were great friends. His father owned a bull and cart and would give me a lift home sometimes from school.

That evening I was too excited to sleep. I wanted to tell Dadi all the details of my trip. I must have told her umpteen times how Princess Margaret looked and how the crowd shouted when we all saw her for the first time standing on that jeep, waving at us while holding a white handbag in her folded left arm. Ma was not interested in my tales. Even my siblings were unwilling to listen to me. But Dadi was happy I'd had an experience of a lifetime.

Chapter Eleven

I was twelve years old when I passed my sixth standard with an average grade, two As, one B and two Cs, which meant I did not receive the scholarship I'd dreamt of. To be eligible for the government scholarship I would have had to obtain the minimum grade of five As. None of the village children managed to obtain the scholarship with the exception of Dinesh, the rich boy who had given me the pair of shoes to play football. Although I knew it was impossible for me to gain the scholarship, I was naturally very disappointed. I envied Dinesh for his achievement, but at the same time felt very pleased for him.

Dinesh had invited me to his celebration party, and I felt very proud that I was the only one from our class to receive an invitation card. The great event was to take place on a Sunday lunchtime. Ma had washed my only decent khaki shorts and white shirt. I borrowed a pair of flip-flop sandals from one of my friends and with great trepidation walked the one mile to his big house. At first the gatekeeper refused to let me in, because my name was not on his list. He did not believe I could be one of the guests as, according to him, only close relatives were invited to the event.

When I was eventually shown in, it was a momentous time for me, because I recalled the occasions when Dadi and I could only peer at the house through the metal gate. Yet here I was being ushered inside. Once inside I was taken aback by the sight of the guests. All of them were immaculately dressed. The ladies were clothed in beautiful saris and matching blouses. The men were all in evening suits, even though the event was taking place at lunchtime and we had soaring temperatures outside. I could not believe my eyes when I saw the boys. They were dressed in cream-coloured long trousers, and nearly all were wearing bow ties. My friend came running to me when he saw me. He had a big smile on his face. He got hold of my right hand and dragged me over to his friends to introduce me. I held him back and told him that I was not appropriately dressed for the occasion. I desperately wanted to run home.

'Oh, don't worry Jaysingh. Nobody cares about how you're dressed.'

But I did. I stood out in my shorts and short sleeve shirt. I became very conscious of my ill-fitting flip-flops and wanted to return home and disappear from the scene. But my friend insisted I should stay and meet his cousins, who had come from various towns in Mauritius, and sought the attention of the boys.

'This is Jaysingh, my school friend. He is a brilliant footballer. He plays with bare feet.'

He quickly related to them the occasion when I could not play with the shoes on that he had given me and how I nearly scored two great gaols when I threw the shoes away. They all laughed loudly at the narrative. I felt like an animal in a zoo, being stared at by these rich, pampered boys. They stopped in their tracks and just stared at me from top to bottom. Their staring eyes made it clear to me that I did not belong there. I felt like an imposter. I was soon ignored amidst the great commotion as my friend prepared to cut his celebratory cake. The cake was massive. Suddenly, everybody started singing Rama's mantra and clapping their hands.

When later I was introduced to my friend's father, he was not very pleased to see me. He wanted to know the name of my Papa and the grades I'd obtained. When I told him, he told me I should have worked harder like his son. I did not tell him I was not as lucky as his son to obtain private tuition from several teachers and live in an environment conducive to reading and studying. Still, when I left my friend's place with that delicious piece of cake, I was the proudest boy in the village. It was a great learning moment of my life, and I did wish him the best of luck in his new school.

Dinesh held my hands and accompanied me to the gate. He promised me he would always stay in touch, no matter what our circumstances were in future. To be fair to him he did. But later I severed the friendship for many reasons. I could not bear the class differences of our livelihood. His name and the sight of him reminded me of all the good things in life that I did not have. But I never hated him for who he was. In fact, I was very proud to have gained his friendship for so long. I learned a lot from him.

Without a scholarship secondary schooling was out of the question for me, as my brother was still completing his Cambridge School Certificate. My mother had enough problems finding money for his schooling and at the same time ensuring that all of us were adequately fed. It was a very unfair world. A world in which, if you were rich like my friend

Dinesh, one could win a scholarship by having an environment where studying was made easy by having all the facilities on hand. My rich friend had admitted many times to me that he was a lucky boy. He only had to concentrate on his study. He did not have to worry about getting up at four in the morning to cut grass for the animals or worry if he would receive adequate food at his next meal.

January was the time when entrance to college usually took place. I was still hopeful my mum would somehow be able to find money and send me to a college as well. There was great excitement among my peers in the village. Most of my friends who passed the sixth standard were boasting with pride of going to the fee-paying colleges in Port Louis. At that time there were different types of secondary college. Most of the colleges accepted students according to their performance in sixth standard, and streamed them accordingly. However, there were some second-rate colleges that were fully independent and accepted pupils only on their ability to pay. Though I knew in my own heart there was no way my mum would be able to afford to pay my fees, I begged her many times, stressing that my future lay in attending college and obtaining a good education as my Dadi kept instilling in me. But the reality of the economic situation was glaringly apparent to me. Ma made me sit down one morning, when I'd asked her for the hundredth time whether I was going to school, having seen one of my village friends being measured for their uniform at the local tailor's shop. She held both of my hands and in a soft voice explained our situation.

'My Jaysingh beta, you cannot go to secondary school because we have no money to fund you. When your brother passes his School Certificate examination, I will give you the chance to go to school.'

'But, Ma, by that time I will forget what I have learnt at the primary school.'

Dadi equally assured me I had to be patient. 'Let your brother finish his education. When he passes his School Certificate examination, you will definitely attend a college.'

I was a confused and desperate little boy. I blamed fate for being born into a poor household. I had promised my friends in the village that I was definitely going to school with them. We had so many rich relatives, yet none of them volunteered to help me. I felt abandoned. I thought it was a cruel world. I begged Ma to borrow money from her rich cousins, but she did not think that was the right thing to do.

Ma informed me the next day, that just for a short duration, she had found a paid job for me. I was to accompany her every day to work in the sugarcane fields for the local white landlord. The pay was one rupee and twenty-five cents per day, around ten pence in today's money. Instead of receiving my precious secondary schoolbooks and a satchel, Ma gave me a pioche and a small, lightweight, shiny black machete with which to plant and cut sugarcane. I could not console myself when I received them. I remember crying nearly all night. Ma kept reassuring me with the same words I had heard before:

'Once your brother finishes his Cambridge School Certificate, you will definitely have your turn to go to a secondary school. In the meantime, you have to work and help the family.'

I looked at Dadi who was sitting nearby gently banging her wooden cane against the cow dung plastered wall, with dismay. She looked at me and beckoned me to sit near her. I walked over to her in an angry mood.

'It's not fair,' I said. 'All my friends are going to school and you want me to work as a labourer. How can I become a teacher planting sugarcane for the white landlords? I am going to remain a poor boy while my friends will enjoy a life of luxury. How am I going to face them in the village? You always taught me that education is paramount for one's success in life. Well?'

Dadi tapped her cane on the cow dung floor loudly three times indicating that I must sit down next to her. She deliberately took her time and after banging her cane another three times against the wall she at last spelled it out.

'At this moment we are a very poor family, my dear boy. You have no choice. We are not going to remain in such a state as you perceive. Mark my word; you will have your chance one day. Always remember what the fortune teller has told you.'

Tears running down my cheeks, I ran from the house and stayed in the neighbouring fields, as I had done previously, until hunger forced me homeward. It was true I had no choice. We were, after all, a very poor family. There were six of us relying heavily on Ma's labours and Dadi's small old age pension. I did not have a father, as all my friends had. Their fathers were bringing money home every week, as most of them were employed in the sugarcane fields. It was a desperate situation. In the end I accepted my position stoically. I decided that there was no point moaning and whingeing anymore. I accepted that God had created my fate. I trusted my Karma and Dadi that surely my time would come one day. From then on, I stopped crying and swore that I would never show my real feelings to anybody, not even to Dadi.

The day before I was to start my life as a labourer, I had a wash and went to our local temple with a bunch of marigolds. I prostrated in front of the tall statue of Hanumanji and prayed for my future. I sought His Lordship's help to show me the path whereby I would not stay permanently as a labourer and would one day be able to go school.

On the coming Monday, when most of my close friends were getting ready to go to school, I had to get up at six in the morning to prepare myself for the life of a labourer. Ma had already prepared my lunch, which consisted of the previous night's left-over roti and aubergine curry. I picked up my pioche and the small machete, instead of pencils and paper, and made my way to the appointed destination on my own. On that day I would have done anything not to walk that muddy road of the village but, unfortunately, that was the only way to the fields. I was resolved not to talk to anybody. I even failed to greet the Elders who were sitting at the crossroads, an act which was seen as most disrespectful in the village. One of my chachas, who was crouching among the group, suddenly got up. I could see him from the corner of my eye. As was his custom he called my name in his soft, lingering voice.

'Jaysingh beta, where are you going at this time of the day?'

'I'm going to work, Chacha. It's a great day for me. I'm going to earn money to support our family.' I shivered at my own reply.

'But I thought you were going to school with my Rahen. He is going to Port Louis High School,' he queried with a smile, practically shaking both his cheeks.

I looked directly into his eyes and did not say a word, and having steadied my pioche on my shoulder, just walked on, controlling my anger.

It was not only the sarcastic remarks of the Elders that I had to cope with, but the vile chanting of my own school friends that I found most humiliating. Normally I was able to avoid them. They usually walked to the bus stop, on their way to school, at around half past seven in the morning. And, by that time I was already in the field.

However, on one particular day I was late going to work because Dadi was not well. It so happened that as I was passing by, I met a group of my old friends dressed in their school uniforms and on their way to school. I wanted to hide and disappear from the earth when I saw them. I was of course wearing my labourer's clothes, with my pioche on my shoulder. They came running towards me, laughing and sneering.

'Oh, how heavy is your pioche, Jaysingh? You look so dark. Do you know whether you will ever be going to school?'

'I'm sure working in the field is easier than reading books,' one of them said. 'At least you don't have to take examinations. I wish I were earning some money instead of going to school.'

I wish we could have swapped places. I just gave them a wry smile and walked on with the pioche that was charting my life history.

Chapter Twelve

It was the sugarcane planting season, and many of the villagers, men and women whom I knew very well, were there when I arrived at the appointed destination. But most importantly my boyhood friend, Bhardoj, had been seen among the group. Since I had kept what I was doing a secret, all the village labourers were surprised to see me. They stood there, hands on waist and eyes following my every movement. One of the chachas asked why I was not at school, as his own son went to school that morning.

'Ma has no money to send me to school, Chacha.'

I wanted to tell the truth. What was the point of misleading the Elders or anybody else? I wanted to convince myself above all that I had fallen to the bottom of the pit and there was nothing to be ashamed about. I wanted to face the truth with dignity and did not care anymore what others thought of me or my family.

'I will go to school when I have saved enough money. Until then I do not mind working as a labourer. You have to show me the ropes, Chacha.'

'No problems, Jaysingh beta. But you should have gone to school.'

'No, Chacha, school is not for me at present. It is for those boys who can afford to pay the school fees. Besides, I am happy to be with you earning some money for my future.'

What future had I as a labourer I wondered, as I twisted the truth and hid my inner feelings of shame? When at last

Bhardoj saw me, he came running towards me. He hugged me and lifted me in the air.

'Great, Jaysingh, I am so glad to see you here. I told you school is no good for you. School is for those who are lazy and want to waste their time reading stupid books. There are so many things to learn in the fields up here. How we plant sugarcane and how sugar is made. I am going to teach you. You stay close to me. Don't be frightened by the foreman. I'll teach you how to deal with him.'

Bhardoj had been working on and off for the sugarcane company for nearly three years. He had always hated school. To him nature was the best teacher. Once he had tried to go to school, but spent most days absconding. His father had left his mum for a woman in Port Louis when Bhardoj was only five years old. Therefore, like me, he had no father to guide him. Bhardoj's older brother worked as a labourer in another part of the village. He was completely illiterate, like most villagers, and could only sign his name by making a cross. At least Bhardoj was able to sign his name slowly.

Despite our differences, I was attached to Bhardoj. His genuine greeting and hug brought half a smile to my face. I knew he was sincerely sorry for me. And when he later patted my back with his large muscular arms, I was not sure whether I should cry or laugh about the situation I was in.

Every morning the foreman divided the cohort of labourers into different groups. One group was to clear away the dry leaves from the mature sugarcane before it was harvested. This was done by hand. Another group was allocated to cut the mature sugarcane and load it onto the cart, which would be pulled by a bull. The third group, which consisted mainly of women and children, was to plant sugarcane in another part of the field. The job of the final group was to irrigate the sugarcane lanes with water that was pumped through huge plastic pipes from a deep well.

On my first day I was told by the foreman that, since I was a novice labourer, it was a good idea for me to stay with the group that was planting sugarcane. My first job consisted of carrying a full basket of twelve-inch sugarcane cuttings on my head to the six-inch-deep lanes, freshly dug by the adult labourers with their sharp pioches. Every morning two carts full of unripe sugarcane were brought to the site. It was the job of two adults to cut the cane into twelve-inch pieces with their sharp machetes. If at any time the piece got split the foreman would shout at them because that piece had to be thrown away.

'You idiots. Has your mother not shown you how to cut a cane? You illiterate lot. Do I have to show you everything? If you do it again, I will have to deduct your wages.'

'He always behaves like the white farmers,' Bhardoj said in a hushed voice.

The foreman, although he lived in the same village, was unforgiving when anyone made mistakes. He was a tall muscular man with a piercing voice, and one could hear him shouting for miles. He walked with long strides and was always in brown khaki trousers and shirt. Despite the blazing sun in the sky, he never wore a hat.

Once I'd carried my basket to the freshly dug lanes, I had to take the twelve-inch canes, one at a time, and carefully place them diagonally about six inches apart. Each lane was about one hundred metres long, and my daily task was to plant at least five such lanes. Once the canes were placed in the lane, they had to be sprinkled by hand with ammonium sulphate fertilizer and covered by hand with the freshly dug soil. The basket was quite heavy, but I soon got used to the load.

Somehow, Bhardoj managed to become part the group I was in. Since he was two years older than me, he was taller and stronger. He could run to and from the cutting points twice as fast as I could, and was always first to finish his work schedule. He helped me by carrying my basket and placing the canes along the lane.

We worked from seven in the morning until five in the afternoon from Monday to Friday. On Saturday we usually worked until twelve o'clock. Sunday was a rest day. Although, the work was hard and tiring, particularly, in the baking heat of the afternoon, it was often fun just being with Bhardoj. Every day he would devise some sort of mischief to lighten our workloads. I remember the occasion when Bhardoj, with a big grin on his face, explained to me the reason why he always completed his allocated work of five lanes before everybody else.

'Jaysingh, my friend, this is a different type of school. You must not work that diligently. Your work is not going to be marked by a teacher. You must learn the principles of deceit. The white landlord is fat enough due to our arduous labours. He has become rich by ensuring we sweat for the cents that he is giving us. You have to learn the trade of subversion. Do exactly what I'm doing. Otherwise, you will wear yourself out. You are not going to get paid if you become ill. I had to beg him for an unpaid day off when my Dadi died.'

From that day Bhardoj and I, in great secrecy, started planting the cane pieces two feet apart instead of the mere six inches we were told to do. For five days we just loitered along the lanes pretending to be busy. Since we did not have to carry that many baskets, and were always the first ones to complete our work, we often sat on the pile of large, volcanic boulders chatting and waiting for our mothers to complete their methodical work.

On the sixth day, at the end of our shift, the foreman indicated to us that he wanted to show us something. In an excited mood we followed him until he approached the area where we had just completed our work.

'Well, my sons. I cannot understand how you have both managed to complete your work so quickly for the last five days. I hope you have not been cheating,' he said, sarcastically.

'No, Chacha, we have been working very hard,' Bhardoj replied very quickly, pointing towards the lanes that we had just completed.

'Well then, let us see what you have been doing. Can you Jaysingh uncover this lane for the next ten feet and let me see how hard you have both worked today?'

I looked at Bhardoj, but he was whistling as if he had done nothing wrong. It was my lane. Later on, the foreman asked Bhardoj to uncover his lanes. We were caught red-handed. Somebody from the group must have told him what we were doing, because he hardly ever visited our patch. Perhaps the presence of our mothers was the root factor of his shyness. He punished us though. We had to replant all the lanes that we had badly sown. This meant that we lost six days' pay. From then on, we were separated. I was despatched to the group that was cutting sugarcane and loading it into the carts, whereas dear Bhardoj was sent to the irrigation section, which was a lonely job.

The sugarcanes were at least eight to ten feet long. Our job was to slice the cane from its root and divide it into three pieces. Once the canes were cut, we had to load them into the cart which was then taken by the bull to the local sugar factory. This mode of transport was later replaced by petrol driven lorries. Loading the canes into the cart or lorry was quite risky. We had to climb an eighteen-inch-wide ladder, carrying a load of canes on our shoulder, and dump the canes into the cart or lorry until it was full. It took us at least two hours to fill a lorry. We also had to make sure any dry leaves were removed before the canes were taken away to the factory. We were paid by the number of lanes we had cut. By this time, I was earning two rupees a day, which was a good wage for my age. I never missed a day's work and was always punctual.

One day I was quite suddenly transferred to the irrigation section. The foreman did not give any reasons for his action.

As I mentioned before, it was a lonely job. I was hoping to find Bhardoj, but he was nowhere to be seen. I was told later that he had been transferred to the sugarcane cutting and loading section. I was disappointed, as I needed a friendly face to cheer me up.

My first job before irrigating the sugarcane fields was to start the petrol pump that was housed near a deep well. I had to pull the starter cord really hard. As I was not very strong, sometimes it took ages for the engine to kick into action. There were no sprinklers. There were hundreds of long plastic tubes stacked in one place. I had to carry the plastic tubes and connect them to direct the water to the sugarcane lanes. Once the lanes appeared wet, I had to connect another tube and so on until both lanes are completely watered. Sometimes I was told to irrigate the freshly planted canes. At other times I had to water the four-foot-high sugarcanes.

During this time, since there was nobody around apart from the foreman who visited the site once a day, I was left alone. At such times, I often thought of my friends who were at school studying for their examinations and my fate as a labourer. To alleviate my pain, I would loudly sing some of my favourite Hindi songs. One such song was by the famous singer Mukesh: *Chhoti si ye zindagani teri* from the film *Aah.* The song typified my life at that time. It encapsulated the reality that life is very short and one's youth does not last long. The singer pined to reach his beloved place to meet his loved one, away from his lonely and desolate environment. In my case, I wanted desperately to leave behind the labourer's job and search for the opportunity to get an education, just like my school friends.

Another song I would frequently sing was a very sad song by Pradeep:

Pinjare ke panchi re
Tera dard na jaane koi
Bahar se to khamosh re hai tu
Hay e bhitar bhitar roi

The song relates to a caged bird, kept in an unnatural environment. According to the singer, human beings are immune to the suffering of the caged bird. It looks docile and happy, but inwardly, surely, it suffers and wishes to be outside. The bird cannot tell its true story to anyone as it shares the world with human beings whose hearts are made of stone.

Nearly every day, while I was toiling as a labourer, I felt caged in the sugarcane fields. I was suffering horribly inside but there was nobody up there to listen to me and rescue me from the incessant pain I was in. The songs of Pradeep and Mukesh would lift my spirit and keep me sane.

Every time I sang those songs, I could not help but cry and sob. One day the foreman saw me sitting by the sugarcane lanes crying my heart out. He placed his soothing hand on my shoulder.

'What's the matter Jaysingh?'

'Oh, Chacha. I'm very unhappy. I want to go to school, but Ma does not have money. I do not know what to do.'

He held me for a while, speechless and uttered the following words slowly, placing great weight to each word. 'Make sure the lanes are properly watered before you go home.'

He could not bear to look at me from then on. He hardly checked whether I had watered the lanes or not. I could tell he was sympathetic to my plight, but there was nothing he could do.

Chapter Thirteen

My constant companion during my first two years working as a labourer was my dear friend Bhardoj. Although on most days I thought he was a bad influence on me, it was impossible to shake his friendship. He followed me everywhere. On our days off, one of our pursuits was to catch chameleons in the fields. They are a variety of lizard, normally about eight inches in length with a long tail. In the fields we saw only two varieties: green and brown. Bhardoj was mainly interested in the brown type. Although these lizards were very quick at climbing trees and could run quite fast on the ground, somehow Bhardoj was able to catch them with his bare hands.

I was scared of them. I did not like their rolling big, brown eyes and their long, slender tongue. Once a lizard was caught, Bhardoj would wrap it in a cloth. My job was to hold it with both my hands very tightly while my friend lit a cigarette and pushed it into the lizard's mouth. He would then tie its hind legs with string and hang the animal from a branch. The poor lizard would puff the cigarette for hours while we sat in the shade of a tree and watched it getting more and more bloated until it became lifeless. It was a very cruel activity, and although I knew this, it was too enticing to abandon. It was a game at the expense of an innocent animal that had, as I know now, the same right to live in those wild fields as us. But sadly, our knowledge of animal rights was poor.

Cats were detested by the villagers and viewed as evil. They were considered omens of impending disaster, particularly if they happened to cross your path. Hardly any of the villagers owned a cat. But somehow there were wild cats roaming about in the fields and surviving on mice and lizards. However, nearly every house had a dog. They were not seen as pets but kept as guard dogs. In developed countries most dogs are kept indoors, but in our village, they were kept outdoors. They slept mainly in the yard outside the house. Interestingly these dogs ate the same food as the household. If a family was a vegetarian, so was the dog.

I would also spend time at Bhardoj's place, helping my friend to cook his special dishes. He was a great cook. We could only do this activity when his Mum had gone somewhere. He knew exactly where his mum had hidden potatoes, onions and flour. He was told off many times about using this produce, as it was the week's supply. But we were always hungry.

At least once a fortnight I would get the signal that my chachee would not be at home. Bhardoj's job was to prepare some dough while I peeled the onions and cut the potatoes very thinly. He then fried the onion and potatoes in a lot of oil. I had to ensure that the log fire remained constantly at a set temperature while he made two thick roti. When the cooking was finished, we would create a wrap with potatoes, onions and green chillies. Oh, boy, it was so delicious that we could have eaten four roti each. Although Bhardoj never washed his hands prior to making the dough, I never gave any thought to hygiene. We just enjoyed the food like two princes sitting by a log fire. When Chachee found out about our surreptitious activity, we were told off. She would seek the help of Dadi to berate us. And even though I was caned every time, Bhardoj's friendship and the delicious food were too tantalising for me to stop.

Hindi movies were very popular at that time. They were shown at our local cinema. Bhardoj would steal money from his Mum's purse so that he could go to the movies. One Sunday afternoon there was a famous film by Rajkapoor being shown. He asked me to come with him but I had no money. I did not want to squander my precious rupees on cheap entertainment.

'No problem, Jaysingh, I shall pay for your ticket.

Everywhere in the village and the fields, people were talking about the quality of the film. In the end I resigned myself to joining Bhardoj. I did not realise that Bhardoj had devised a scheme. At the ticket counter he bought only one ticket.

'Where is my ticket?' I asked in an amazed tone.

'This is your ticket, Jaysingh. Now as you know there are three intervals when they sell ice cream. At the first interval you come out and hand me your ticket when it will be my turn to go in. At the third interval it will be your turn to see the end of the film.'

'But Bhardoj, I won't know what happened while you are watching.'

'Ah, no problem, I'll fill you in on the scenes that you have missed and you will do the same thing. It is a clever plan. Don't you think so? It is exciting, Jaysingh. Thus, with one ticket we shall watch the whole film.'

'But we could get caught, Bhardoj.'

'Oh no, we won't.'

Bhardoj and I were very proud of our scheme and, since we did not get caught, we repeated it several times.

We never went to work on public holidays and Sundays. Since football was a very popular sport, we spent most of our time playing it and watching the local teams. Football matches were often held between northern village teams in the afternoon. A Pamplemousse team, Jagriti Rovers, had become famous, as it was unbeaten for ten matches. Most of their players were Hindus. One public holiday the team were going to play their nearest rival whose players were all Muslims. Since I was very keen on football, Bhardoj did not have to use his guile to persuade me to join him in watching the match. He just had to assure me that he had the money to pay for the match ticket.

The Jagriti Rovers football ground was about two miles from our village. The road was flanked by sugarcane and vegetable fields. As we were walking, Bhardoj's eagle eye noticed that one of the fields was covered with ripe watermelons.

'Are you hungry, Jaysingh?'

'Yes. I'm famished. Have you got some bread in your pocket?'

'No. I have better dish than that. Can you see those big juicy watermelons in that field? We are going to take two of them for our dinner.'

‘But that is stealing, Bhardoj. Dadi said stealing is a bad thing. God will punish us.’

‘No Jaysingh. The farmer is not going to miss two melons. Can’t you see he has thousands of them in the field? Besides, God is bound to forgive us since we are going to take just two of them.’

‘But Bhardoj, what will happen if Ma finds out. There is a hut in the middle of the field Bhardoj. The guard may be hiding in it.’

‘You just follow me and do exactly as I tell you. The guard won’t even see us.’

Like a tiger we crawled on our hands and feet. When we came within the sight of the hut, Bhardoj signalled me to flatten myself on my belly. In that belly position we slithered forward like snakes until we reached the melons. They were huge and heavy. Bhardoj signalled me to turn on my back and shift myself to the exit position. He picked one of the biggest melons and gently placed it on my stomach. He picked another one and placed it on his belly. In that supine position, with water melons on our bellies, we quietly crept backwards until we reached the road. Fortunately, there was nobody around to see us, and we got away with two ripe watermelons and only had to smash them on a boulder to savour the pink flesh.

That was not the end of our adventure on that day. With our bellies full with watermelon, we slowly, dancing and singing, made our way to the football match. The match had already started. We could hear the roaring sounds of the crowd, and I was anxious to get into the ground as soon as possible. The entrance gate was still open and I could see late spectators were buying their tickets. Bhardoj suddenly dragged me by my hand and uttered in a hushed voice that we were not going to buy tickets.

'There is a gap in that iron sheet fencing. We just have to prise open the tinfoil to access the ground.'

'Oh no, Bhardoj. You promised me you were going to buy the match ticket. I do not want to be caught and go to prison.'

'Sorry, Jaysingh, I forgot to bring my money. Do you have any?'

'No, I don't.'

I started losing my temper as every second meant that I was missing the match. In the end, in desperation, I followed Bhardoj like a dog. We walked at least three hundred feet along the iron sheet fencing of the ground to a point where the huge swinging branches of mango trees hid us from the entrance gate. Bhardoj used his brute force and prised out an iron sheet that appeared to be only loosely nailed to the wooden upright. His action made a loud clanking noise, and I wanted to run away. But Bhardoj grabbed me and showed me a twenty-four-inch hole through which I could see the grounds. He wriggled through the hole then signalled for me to do the same. I thrust my head through the hole, but when I lifted my head, instead of seeing the smiling face of Bhardoj I saw two bulky men holding him firmly by his hands. One of the men had clasped his huge palm over Bhardoj's face. The sight of the men terrified me so much that I started weeping very loudly. My body was shaking violently and I was wetting my pants at the same time.

'Well lads. You know that it is wrong to get into the ground without paying. I have to take you both to the police station.'

'No Sir, please, I beg you,' pleaded Bhardoj. 'We are poor children. We had saved our money for months to see the match, and on our way here four boys attacked us and took our money. Jagriti Rovers is our favourite team, and we wanted to somehow see the match. What we have done is wrong. We shall never do such things again.' He clasped both his hands and bowed his head.

'You are both bad boys. Let us see what the ground manager says about your action.'

He took us to the entrance gates. While one of the men was holding our hands firmly, the other brought the manager. He looked us up and down, shook his head.

'You said some boys up here took your money.'

'Yes Sir. They even hit us.' Bhardoj lifted his shirt and showed the red scratch marks on his back. He lifted my shirt and pointed to the pink marks all along my back and the front of my chest. I was sweating with terror.

'Okay, you can stay behind and see the match but in future you should never try to steal yourself in the ground without paying.'

What an escape. Bhardoj was a master of tricks.

That was the last time I ever went to a football match with Bhardoj. I decided that Bhardoj was a liability and was dragging me along the wrong path, which was totally against the teachings of Dadi.

Chapter Fourteen

While I was working as a labourer, Ma allowed me to keep at least two rupees per week for my own use. As I was determined to save enough money, I devised a clever method to hide my savings from my brother. He was renowned for stealing any sum he could lay his hands on. At the back of our house there was a tall coconut tree. Five metres from it there was a large boulder. I decided my savings would be safer underneath the boulder. I placed the coins in a plastic bag and hid the bag deep in a hole underneath the stone. In time I managed to save thirty rupees.

Since my thirst for education had never abated, I decided to spend six rupees per month on private tuition. One of my friends had told me of a teacher who lived near his house and gave private lessons on Sunday mornings. Although the teacher was from the lower caste, I was determined to seek his help. One Sunday morning I made my way to his house. I waited till a group of twelve students had finished their lessons. I introduced myself to the teacher and explained my situation.

'Woogara,' he said, 'You are going to waste your money. You are so much behind in your study. My students are all in form three. Have you studied any of these books?'

He showed me an English grammar book and a French exercise book.

'No sir.'

'Would you be able to do these algebra questions? How can you find time while working as a labourer in the sugarcane fields?'

'I shall try, sir, if you will help me. And I will find time to complete my homework.'

Well, that was the start of my secondary education. From then on, every Sunday morning from nine in the morning till noon, I took lessons in English, Mathematics and French. While the other students were attending fee-paying colleges and topping up their studies with private lessons, I was relying on one three-hour lesson each week for my education. I also had to study another two subjects, as five subjects were the minimum requirements to sit for the GCE O Level. I thought British History and English Literature could form part of the five subjects. My initial plan was to study these two subjects in a year's time.

On Saturday evenings, once fortnightly, I had started to take Hindi lessons, which I enjoyed very much. Mauritius was made up of diverse populations, and the government of the day had started an initiative to encourage the citizens to learn their own language, such as Hindi, Urdu and Chinese. Being a British colony, English was the main language of the Island. But French and Creole were widely spoken in the towns and among the upper classes. In our village we mainly spoke Bhojpuri, a language quite similar to Hindi. At that time, it was easier to become a language teacher. But Bhojpuri was not officially recognised as a language. Since secondary schooling had become a dream to me, I thought that perhaps my in-depth study of Hindi would give me an opportunity to become a Hindi teacher one day.

I was equally determined to pursue my private study. Bhardoj, as usual, laughed at me and thought that I was wasting my precious money for my private lessons, but I ignored his sneers and sarcasm. I managed to purchase the appropriate books from a student at a much-reduced price. His father had suddenly died from cardiac arrest and poor Kam was forced to abandon his study at the fee-paying college in Port Louis. I created a timetable for my study and zealously adhered to it. I read and did most of my homework at night or in the early hours of the morning. My preferred time was at four, as the temperature was bearable and I could concentrate on my study before going to work in the sugarcane fields. Since there was no electricity, I had to use a small tin kerosene lamp with a tiny handle. By the time it was time to go to work, the insides of my nostrils were blackened.

Books were expensive, and as there was no local library, I made a point to enrol myself in the central library of Port Louis. Once a month, on Saturday afternoon, I would visit the library and borrow as many books as I was allowed to take home. Books on British history and English classics like George Eliot's *Silas Marner* and George Orwell's *Animal Farm* were my favourites. Sadly, on those days I had to miss my Hindi lessons.

I read everything that I could lay my hands on. On my way home from my Hindi class I always made a detour to the shops. There I frequently found torn pieces of newspaper and even magazines. Besides the library books, these bits and pieces of newspaper were a very welcome resource for me, as some articles that were topical were written in French and in English. I read every word on every line. Once I had read them, I carefully placed the materials in a wooden box for my future reference. Although I begged my brother to help me with anything that he had read at college, he was never forthcoming and ignored my distress.

At this point of my life, I was a bitter and frustrated young man. I was angry with nearly everybody: with my own plight, with Ma, my brother, my primary school friends, but mostly with the villagers. I was fed up with the caste system that was practised in the village. I remained aloof from the boys of my own age and felt ashamed mixing with them, particularly those who were attending colleges. I was jealous and envied them. I found great comfort by going to the temple at least once a week and praying for my good fortune and the success of my brother in his much-awaited Cambridge School Certificate examination. I would carefully follow every ritual of prayer. I had to have a shower from a small bucket of water to clean myself and, as was the custom, I only drank water. Since I could not afford to buy expensive fruits or incense, I took flowers to give as an offering to my god, Hanumanji, or, during mango season, mangoes from our fruit trees. Although I did not know most of the mantras, I would repeat some of the lines several times quite loudly to ensure that the gods had listened to my request.

On the day my brother was to receive his examination result, Ma and I made an extra visit to the Triolet temple. We made sure that enough time was devoted to each god so that none of them would be offended. Although Vishnu was the mightiest Lord of all gods, I could not help spending more than ample time praying to my favourite god, Hanumanji. I was not ashamed to prostrate on the wet concrete slab in the presence of other worshippers and ask Hanumanji to grant my request.

'Please, God, ensure that my brother will pass his examination. This is the only chance I have got. How can I carry on working in the sugarcane fields? I am too fragile. Please God if you will do this, I will definitely become a lifelong devotee of yours. Please, have pity on me.'

Other devotees could chant special kirtans in a rhythmic way in the presence of Hanumanji, but since I had forgotten most of them while working in the sugarcane fields, I thought at least in my mumbling voice I could reach any gods who could hear me.

On the result day, at around ten o'clock in the morning when the post man brought the long-awaited letter, we all clasped our hands in the praying position as my brother slowly opened the letter. By the expression on his face, we knew he had failed the examination. Out of six subjects he obtained only one pass, and that was in Christianity. I could not believe he failed French, Mathematics, English, English Literature and British History and only managed to obtain a borderline pass in Christianity. I was horrified and dumbfounded. It was a major blow to all of us. Our hopes and aspirations for a better life had suddenly been blown to pieces. We all looked at each other and Ma started crying until she was too tired to cry any longer. I was too shocked and shaken to show any emotion. I wanted to cry like Ma, but my eyes remained dry and my body remained numb. I turned and walked to the back of the house and sat on a boulder in a meditative mood.

I decided to accept my fate with honour, knowing I had to spend another year in the fields. I had dreamt nearly every night that his success in the examination would not only give me the opportunity to attend a secondary school, but most importantly my brother would get a good job and earn money and that would help to improve our standard of living. My sisters would finally be able to wear decent clothes and would no longer be a laughing-stock when visiting our rich cousins.

My trust and admiration for my brother disintegrated within seconds. I felt that he had let us all down. Instead of rescuing us from the plight of poverty and humiliation, he had pushed us into a deeper hole of deprivation forever. Yes, I hated him at that time. I also lost my faith in Hanumanji. I stopped going to the temple and made a solemn oath that I was going to rely on my own strength and ability. I started making greater efforts with my study and continued with my private tuition. I became more determined than ever to study key subjects that would become useful one day should I decide to take my General Certificate of Education (GCE Ordinary Level) examination as a private student.

It was at this time I arranged to meet my rich friend at a secret rendezvous, as we both knew his father would not approve of my meeting him in his house. At this meeting we made an arrangement that once a week we would get together and he would help me with my lessons and revise with me what he had been studying at his own Government State School in Port-Louis. We maintained this relationship for nearly two years. On these occasions he would bring cakes and chocolates and sometimes curry and rice in a tin. I am forever indebted to this friend who helped me so much. In later life he went to England to train as a doctor and became a very successful heart surgeon in Mauritius.

I started planning to take my GCE examination in three years' time which would not require attending college on a full-time or part-time basis. Thus, I continued working as a labourer and with my studies until I was sixteen years old. In the meantime, my brother retook his examination for the second time and failed again, although this time he managed to obtain a pass in British History as well as Christianity.

Chapter Fifteen

The death of my beloved Dadi was a traumatic event in my life. It is difficult to imagine how I coped after she was gone. She was my sun. Ever since I started breathing, she was around. She was always there when I needed her. She was my saviour and also my friend to whom I could relate practically anything.

I was picking small chillies for the Port Louis market with my brother one Sunday, in the field at the back of the house. We were severely strapped for cash. The cow had stopped giving milk and we had to rely heavily on the paltry produce of the land. The chillies were the only items left in the field and were sold to a middleman who would take them to the market. Our concentration was suddenly disturbed by the panting sound of Bhardoj. He was shouting at us that we must return home quickly because our Dadi was very ill. During this time Dadi had become dependent on us for most of her needs. She was bedridden as the woes of advanced diabetes overtook her whole life. She had become blind and had urinary incontinence. There was no money in the house to buy the insulin injections she badly needed. Visits to doctors cost money, and they were sharks preying on the poor. She developed many complications which we were powerless to prevent, including bouts of severe diarrhoea, which at times were impossible to stop. We tried every local remedy, but to no avail. We knew that she was dying and we dreaded that day.

The thoughts of losing Dadi kept me awake nearly every night. I loved her very much, but I was also concerned that we would lose her monthly old age pension at her death. How were we going to survive? Although it was only the tiny sum of twenty rupees (about forty pence) per month, it saved us from starvation. During this dreadful period, we survived mainly on the manioc plants that we had planted at the back of the house. These are hardy plants. They can withstand long periods of dry season and can still produce good size maniocs. Ma stopped serving us even those tiny portions of salted fish. They were reserved for Dadi as the salted fish was the only stimulant left for her to eat something when she became gravely ill.

So, when we heard Bhardoj yelling, my brother and I galloped to her bedside. Dadi's sister and Bhardoj's mum were already there, sitting on the cow-dung floor, chanting Rama's name. My Dadi was lying on the bed that I shared with her every night. Her head was on my mum's lap. Ma was talking to her softly. Ma directed Bhardoj to run to the primary school to fetch our youngest sister, Deomatee, as it was customary for close relatives to be present when someone was dying. Somehow Dadi sensed our arrival and she opened her eyes. With her forefinger she signalled us to approach her. Tears were running down my cheeks as I held her thin wrinkly hand. She looked at me, trying to utter a few words that I could not decipher. Even before my brother could approach her, she had turned her face towards Ma's lap. It was during that moment she passed away. Sadly, by the time Deomatee arrived home, our beloved Dadi was already dead.

The death of my Dadi was a great personal loss to me. I probably felt it more than anybody else because of my closeness to her. I suckled her for many months when I was a baby. She was my everything. I slept with her nearly every night. She protected us against the criticisms of the villagers and particularly of her sisters and our cousins, who were our bitter rivals. Looking back, we were probably saved from dreadful in-fighting because of Dadi's down-to-earth philosophy of life. She always advocated that friendships were more important than living with strife. I remember one day my brother and I were arguing bitterly about something and throwing punches at each other. Dadi called us and asked my brother to fetch a sturdy stick. He had no choice but to obey her. We knew that we were going to be caned. But normally the caning took place when we were not prepared for it and, usually, she used her walking stick. A request of this nature was very unusual. When my brother brought the stick, Dadi asked him to break it. Of course, he could not do so as the stick was rather strong. Then she asked me to do the same. As I was weak and didn't possess the required physical force, my attempt was fruitless. What chance had I when my older brother could not do the honour of breaking the stick? She then asked both of us to break the stick together by applying greater force at the same time. To our great amazement the stick split in the middle. Satisfied and pleased with herself, Dadi asked both of us to explain the rationale for her action, and whether we had learnt anything from the exercise. Well, it became quite plain to me that we could not break the stick by our individual effort, but when we applied equal force at the same time the stick broke.

'Here is a lesson to both of you. You must both learn to live together. If you both work hard without any acrimony, you can achieve a lot. Strife and fights will only weaken your will to make progress in life.'

I think I have been inculcated with this philosophy and have tried to live my life by it. However, over time I have found that an individual's attitudes change through different experiences, and at times it has been difficult to live by that principle.

Dadi was not just a great storyteller; she also knew how to keep us occupied. One day Bhardoj and I were fighting in the yard when Dadi heard our screaming. As soon as we spotted Dadi standing there, leaning on her stick, Bhardoj immediately stopped. She signalled us to her side and made us sit down.

'I dreamt last night that there was some treasure hidden by the side of our house. I heard a loud chinking noise this morning up there, and I want both of you to dig and find that treasure. You have to dig quickly or else the treasure will vanish.'

Bhardoj's eyes brightened with joy. He ran to his house and brought his Mum's pioche. I managed to find a tiny pickaxe. We frantically started digging. Being volcanic soil, the ground was quite soft. We dug and dug for hours, until we were completely drained of energy. We never found the treasure. Often, I wonder if Dadi deliberately misled us or genuinely heard the sound of coins. She was certainly very convincing. The next day we had to refill the holes. Bhardoj was convinced he had heard the noise of coins too and was willing to carry on digging. But Dadi felt it was a waste of time digging further. According to her, the spirit was in no mood to divulge the treasure at that time. She convinced us that some other day the spirit would guide her, and we would be able to find the treasure.

Another event that affected me during this period was the tragic death of Bhardoj's mum, which occurred only few months after the death of my Dadi Her death has always reminded me of the transient nature of life. Even Shakespeare could not have written a better tragedy.

I was, by then, fourteen years old, and was still working in the sugarcane field. I had graduated from planting canes to cutting them and loading the lorries. When I got up that morning, 29 January 1960, there was heavy rain and it was impossible to venture outside without being blown away. Ma advised me to stay at home. This meant I would lose a day's wages when I was saving every cent for my private tuition. None of the villagers possessed a radio at that time, and there was no way of assessing the weather except by looking the changing shapes of the sky and listening to the Elders. I was glad I listened to Ma and stayed at home, because within hours the stormy weather turned cyclonic. The doors and windows of our two-room house started shaking, and the iron sheets that covered the roof were rattling. At this time, nearly all the houses on our road were roofed with sugarcane thatch. Ours was an exception, because it was more recently built and had a wooden frame on a concrete base and a metal roof.

Bhardoj lived opposite our house across the muddy road. They had a three-room thatched house with a long veranda that was supported with a four-foot high, L-shaped stone wall. When the cyclone started raging, with winds reaching 297 kph according to a village teacher, I could see their thatched roof was being blown into the air. Their coconut and jackfruit trees had already been uprooted.

Ma told us to take cover under our wooden bed as the neighbours started pouring into our house. There must have been at least twenty people, all crouched on the floor, praying that our house would not be blown away. There were no facilities to cook. Our tiny wooden kitchen, which was situated outside our house, was already demolished and most of the pots and pans had been broken. Water was everywhere, running like rivers. The cowshed was severely damaged, and I remember Ma begging a male neighbour to bring the cow into the room where we were all huddled. Poor chap, despite lashing rain, the howling of the stormy winds, and the doors and windows flapping, he bravely managed to bring our cow, Ramu, and the three precious goats safely inside.

The presence of our animals spurred our chachee, Bhardoj's mum, to slip quietly to her house to check on the safety of her only goat. In the commotion, nobody even noticed she had left the house. The next thing we saw was

Chachee pulling her goat by a string towards our house. But the wind was too fierce. It was blowing from all angles. It kept blowing her away, and at one point she fell to the ground, the goat freed from her grip. We shouted at her to return but, instead, she ran and took shelter under her veranda.

I can still see her anguished face sometimes in my dreams. She kept peering at us through the lashing rain and waving at us. She tried again to trace her steps back to our house, but the violent wind again defeated her. One moment she was there and the next she disappeared under her house which suddenly collapsed like a pack of cards. We all gasped with horror. Despite the torrential rain and violent wind, most of us rushed to the house and started shouting for her and pulling at the roof with our bare hands. We had no idea where she was, but after ten minutes of desperate searching we managed to find her. She was covered with water, apparently drowned. With tears in our eyes, we brought her into our house and laid her on the only bed. Ma pronounced that she was already dead. While the males sat on their knees with their heads bowed, praying to heavenly gods, the ladies removed her wet clothing and wrapped her in Ma's best white sari.

Since the storm raged for two days non-stop, we hardly ate. We just drank the rainwater and curled ourselves in any place that we could find. Some of us were even lying next to the decomposing body of our chachee. A corner of one of the rooms was designated as a latrine. The smell of the defaecation, urine and the decomposing body permeated our senses, but we all accepted our fate stoically. This was a storm that will always stay in my memory as a time when the caste system was forgotten, when the survival of everybody, including the animals, became paramount. We supported each other and bonded together like a family in our common grief for the loss of our beloved chachee. She was cremated during the eye of the cyclone, and we heard subsequently that another forty people had died in the country and 41,000 inhabitants had become homeless. My family was very lucky to remain alive during the disastrous Cyclone Carol.

Chapter Sixteen

After working nearly two years as a labourer I became very disenchanted with my life. I became rather depressed, particularly while I was working in the irrigation section. The more I sung those sad songs, the more I felt I was not going anywhere with my life. The future looked very bleak.

'You are not going to work as a labourer anymore,' Ma said to me one day. 'You are going to learn a trade.'

'What trade, Ma?'

'You are going to Saint Paul to learn to be a draper.'

'Does this mean I have to live at Saint Paul away from you?'

'Yes.'

Dadi was dead and I was totally fed up with my life generally. I thought learning a trade was better than working as a labourer in the sugarcane fields. I was thus shunted to Saint Paul to live with my rich cousins, who I detested because of their wealth. The eldest brother was engaged in merchandise commerce. He imported all types of fabrics from India and would sell them from different markets in the Curepipe area of Mauritius and privately to French ladies in their houses. Every morning, with the aid of a helper, the son of his eldest sister, he would load his big white van with hundreds of different fabric rolls and drive to different places. The family had become very rich through this trade, because of the booming market he had created for his goods.

Ma had persuaded my cousin to show me the business of merchandise trading. It was agreed that I would not be paid while I was learning, as I was lodging and boarding with them. Suddenly, I was thrown into a world where there was running water, electric lighting and indoor and outdoor toilets. The family had two cars, a telephone and a radio. I remember the day when the telephone rang, not realising where exactly the sound emanated from, I ran from the room thinking that some sort of ghost had invaded the house. For the first time I saw a gas-fired stove with four rings set up in a large purpose-built kitchen. For breakfast we would eat a whole roll of fresh bread with cheese and butter. My standard of living was transformed overnight from pauper to prince. I could not believe my luck.

I was taken to a shop in Curepipe where my eldest cousin who had employed me bought a pair of shorts, a long-sleeved shirt and a pair of blue flip flops. Every morning, after the delicious breakfast, I would move the requisite rolls of fabric from the house to the van with the helper and, in the evening, we would unload them and bring them back. After the van was loaded, my cousin would drive the van to a set destination, with me sitting at the back of the van on top of the fabric whilst the helper, who was my senior, sat in the front of the van next to my cousin. This ritual never changed for the whole duration of my stay.

Quite frequently, we would drive to French houses where, for the first time, I came face to face with French ladies, their husbands and sometimes their children. While working as a labourer I was scared of them. Here, when I said '*Bonjour Madame*', they would respond to my greetings. On such occasions, the helper and I would bring the fabric rolls as identified by my cousin to their lounges, where I saw furniture of exquisite quality. They had marbled floors and beautiful rugs. What amazed me most was that their dogs lived in their houses like their owners. They had cats too which were seen sometime sitting on the laps of the ladies. Once I had delivered the rolls, I always stayed in the van while the helper and my cousin conducted the sales transaction. I was not to be present on such occasions. So, I was learning nothing about the trade of selling and the finer points of business.

The first evening at my cousin's place, I wanted to use the toilet facilities, but I felt ashamed to use the indoor toilets. I thought my cousins, two boys and three girls, would smell my poo. Moreover, I did not think it was proper to relieve oneself in the house; I had always done such things in the fields. I did not realise I had to pull the chain, since nobody had shown me how to flush a toilet with running water. I was so frightened of those sophisticated gadgets that I ran outside and relieved myself at the back of their garden behind a tree. For three days I maintained this routine. On the fourth day I was caught in the act by my youngest cousin. He started calling me a savage and the monkey of Triolet. Very soon the news of my misdemeanour spread to the whole house. It was only my fourth day away from my village home, and my naivety about that different world was so glaring, I would have run home had I known the way. From that day onwards I knew I did not belong there. Their world seemed too sophisticated for my liking.

After a few months of travelling in the back of the van and moving those long heavy fabric rolls to and from the French dwellings, I started becoming disenchanted with my new life. What hurt me most during this period was that while I was in servitude to my cousin, albeit he was supposed to be teaching me the nuances of fabric trading, I could not bear the thought of not going to college. Every morning I watched my two male cousins preparing themselves to go to their respective colleges. They were always immaculately dressed; they even wore brown ties and carried heavy brown leather school bags. In the evening, after a long day's work, I was tired and had to go bed early to recover for the next day's trip. While I was sent to bed the two boys were shut in a special study room where they spent their time reading and doing their homework. On many occasions I wanted to be with them, but was told by my eldest cousin I must not disturb them and must never visit that room.

One day I could not go to work owing to a very bad cold. My Mowsee (Ma's female cousin) thought I had pneumonia, as I had quite a high temperature. She sponged me with tepid water and told me to stay in bed. Around ten o'clock in the morning I was feeling much better and decided it was time to investigate my cousins' study room. Slowly I crept along the corridor and accessed their study. I could not believe my eyes when I saw all those books carefully lined up on long bookshelves. There was a large rectangular table with at least six chairs and two table lamps. On each side of the table, I could visualise my two cousins seated, studying in silence and doing their homework. I sat on one of the chairs and carefully opened an exercise book. I could see that my cousin was doing very well, because there were red ticks everywhere. While I was immersed in my surreptitious act, my Mowsee caught me.

'Here you are, Jaysingh. Why are you out of bed?'

'I am feeling a lot better now, Mowsee. I wanted to see some of the books my cousins are reading. I am amazed to see so many books.'

'Don't disturb their exercise books. Those are ready for their private tuition this evening.'

I did not realise until then that my two cousins not only went to a renowned college, they were also topping up their education with private tuition. I felt sick at the thought of how my destiny was defined by sheer poverty. I told my Mowsee I wanted to attend college as well and study like my cousins.

'You are learning a trade, Jaysingh. One day you will run your own business.'

How could I be assured of such a destiny when after nearly six months I was still moving the fabric rolls? I was never given the opportunity to speak to any of the clients, and was never taught how the business ran. I had no idea, despite all those months, how he imported those fabrics. I wanted to know the detailed aspects of the import business, but I was left in the dark.

Another event that finally made my decision to return to my village was the day when there was great excitement in the house. All my cousins and Mowsee were busy getting dressed in their best clothes and I was told to do the same.

'We are going to see Father Christmas, Jaysingh. We are all going to Curepipe this evening.'

'Who is Father Christmas?' I asked my youngest cousin.

'Who is Father Christmas? Jaysingh does not know.'

He mimicked my question so loudly that everybody could hear him. At this juncture all the children and even the adults started laughing and giggling in concert. I could not understand the reason for their laughter and just stared at them in silence.

'Have you not celebrated Christmas, Jaysingh, when you were a little boy?' Mowsee asked me gently

'No,' I said ashamedly.

'Don't worry, beta. You are going to see him tonight in the shop,' my Mowsee said quietly, hugging me tightly with both her arms.

'Christmas day is a very special day for the Christians, and they celebrate the day in a strange way.'

The streets of Curepipe were sparkling with multicoloured flashing and twinkling lights. All the shops were decorated. It was the first time in my thirteen years of life that I had seen such a beautiful sight. We went from one shop to another until suddenly my eldest cousin pointed to a red and white figure.

'There is Father Christmas. You can ask him anything and he will give it to you.'

'Will he?' I asked in amazement, looking at my Mowsee. I could see all my cousins had great difficulty in containing their laughter.

'Go and ask him whatever you want.'

I gingerly made my way to the red figure, who was surrounded by small children. He beckoned me to sit down while my eldest cousin had a quiet word with him. Since I was not very good in conversing in Creole, so when I spoke, I clasped both my hands as if praying to my almighty Hanumanji and spoke in Bhojpuri, the Hindu dialect we spoke in the village.

'Please, Almighty can you give Ma some money so that I can go to the college like my cousins. We are very poor and I desperately want to go to school.'

'Jaysingh, he does not understand Bhojpuri. Tell him in Creole?' My youngest cousin giggled.

I repeated the same requests as best as I could in broken Creole. When I turned my head around everybody was laughing, and even the red figure sitting in front of me was shaking his head. At this point the red figure shifted his white beard in position, and I noticed he was in fact a white man.

It was a game to them. I felt bitter afterwards that I had become a source of entertainment to them. I felt so naive and greatly humiliated.

Years later I wrote the following stanzas that aptly summarised my feelings at that time:

Memories torment me
I must have been thirteen years old
I was staying at my cousins' place
I was the naive poor village boy and they were the rich town ones

We are going to see Father Christmas
They shouted, laughter in their eyes,
dragging me and pushing me to their car
Who is Father Christmas? I asked

There was a roar of laughter, giggles and stares of horror
Here is a stupid boy
Does not know who Father Christmas is
Lives in a village and only knows cows and goats

I sat huddled at the back of the car
Ashamed of my ignorance
Ridiculed for asking
Yet longing to know who was Father Christmas

In a village, with no radio or television
No telephones or cars
Hardly the staple food of manioc and rice
Ever filled the empty belly of a poor village boy

How could I explain to the pompous ones
That you are right I had never heard of Father Christmas
That Father Christmas only appears to the rich
In their imagination when their bellies are full

When Ma came to see me on the following Sunday, I insisted I wanted to come home for New Year. My village was my home where I was comfortable and could freely speak the language that had been passed on to me by my great grandparents without being laughed at. I had had enough of being subservient to my cousins. I refused to return to that luxurious world. The children of this different world thought I was uncivilised, as in their minds being surrounded by materialism was the key ingredient of civilisation. I could not take their laughter and degradation any longer. I preferred to go back and work as a sugarcane labourer rather than supposedly being trained to be a fabric tradesman.

Chapter Seventeen

Ma was so disappointed with my brother's examination result that she finally decided to stop funding his schooling. As he had no academic qualifications, he found great difficulty in finding a job. This was a thorny time for him and the family. While three of his closest friends started work as primary school teachers, my brother was thrown on the unemployment heap without any remorse or sympathy from anybody including our closest relatives.

The only option of employment for him was to work in our one and a half acres of land or as a labourer in the sugarcane fields as I was doing. He was not very keen to dirty his hands as a labourer, so he spent some of his days helping Ma planting tobacco, sweet corn and peanuts on our land. While every morning his friends were going to school, my dear brother was weeding the field with his bare hands and bringing fodder for the animals.

I must admit he was a great help to Ma, and our income did improve slightly because we employed fewer outside labourers. But working as a farmer was no substitute for working in a shiny office of the government or working as a teacher.

The villagers, as they did to me, started making fun of him. I know I hated him for his failure in his examination, but now looking back I cannot help but feel sorry for him. We'd had no male figure in the house, and although Dadi and Ma had tried their best to discipline him and instil in him the importance of study and academic success, he had not developed the steel-like determination and ambition needed to get him successfully through the times we were experiencing.

Ma was already laden with heavy debt having recently married the younger of my two older sisters, Jannee, in an arranged marriage to Moona who lived in Port Louis. Since we were a poor family, it had been a very worrying time for Ma trying to find a suitable husband for my sister. One of our chachas who worked in the Port Louis market managed to find Moona, who was at least nine years older than my sister. The most important element of the arranged marriage was the fact that Moona belonged to the same caste as us and worked as a motor mechanic. The fact that he did not have his own house and lived with his half-brother was of no consequence. Although my sister had the opportunity to meet Moona in the presence of the Elders, according to the custom at that time she did not have the option of refusing Moona. Fortunately, he was a very charming man and travelled on a shiny motor bike. I was glad that Moona married Didi Jannee, because he became some sort of father figure in our house. And since Moona did not have his own mother, as she had died when he was a child, he built a beautiful relationship with Ma.

Despite our financial hardship, Ma kept her promise and decided it was my turn to go to the college. At last, after nearly five years working as a labourer and unsuccessfully learning the merchandise trade with my cousin in Saint Paul, I was given the golden opportunity to attend Port Louis High School at sixteen years old. When Ma gave me the great news, I hugged her and kissed her and, as a gesture of the greatest respect, I knelt down and kissed her feet.

'Ma, thank you. I will study very hard, and I am going to pass my examination and be successful in life. I will improve the sorry plight of our situation.'

It was a promise I was determined to keep. But I knew I still needed the help and blessing of our Saviour. Despite the tentative rejection of my faith in our Lord Hanumanji, I ran to his temple with a bunch of flowers and thanked the Lord for giving me such a chance. I also asked his forgiveness for ignoring him. A school uniform and, for the first time, a pair of blue plimsolls were bought for me. It was strange to wear the college uniform and my own shoes. I did not care how I looked in them. I ran the length and breadth of our back garden until I was completely exhausted. I shouted and screamed towards the sky. At last, I thought to myself, I was no longer going to toil in the fields. I told Bhardoj about the sudden change in my fortune. I showed him my college uniform. He was very pleased for me, but he still felt that schooling was a waste of time.

Following a preliminary entrance examination at Port Louis High School in English, French and Mathematics, I was allowed to join the Form Four students. On my first day, Ma accompanied me to the school. She had taken with her a year's worth of school fees, having recently sold a calf. She insisted she would pay my school fees a year in advance. She made a special arrangement with the Principal – since she was not able to pay monthly school fees regularly, she would pay all outstanding fees in arrears once she sold another calf. The Principal reluctantly agreed. So, my whole schooling was based on the health and wellbeing of our cow and her calf.

In the beginning, I travelled to the college on my bicycle, an eighteen-mile return journey from Port Louis to my village of Mahaswar Nagri in Triolet. There were many small hills, and the main road was narrow and always busy with cars, buses and bullock carts. The majority of the students travelled to their respective secondary schools in Port Louis by bus. I was not lucky enough to experience that luxury, as Ma could not afford to pay my bus fare. The choice was simple, either I used my bicycle or I walked. On the whole I enjoyed the journey. I was young and it was exciting to cycle to school five days a week with another student at the school, Dina, who soon became a close friend. During this time, I did not go to the fields at all, as Ma was determined that I concentrate on my study. I diligently did all my homework each night, and it was one of the happiest times of my life.

Of the three types of secondary school at this time, those pupils who got a mark of ninety and above units in their primary school examination obtained an automatic right to attend the elite government colleges. These colleges were viewed with the same high regard as Oxford and Cambridge. Attendance was free, and students also obtained free books and a special pass to travel by bus. They were seen as the brightest children on the island. Five children from Triolet attended the government college. They hardly mixed with the other children. One such pupil was my rich friend, who had obtained the top mark of ninety-eight units in his primary school examination. He never travelled by bus, because his father would take him to school every morning in his red Citroën car.

The second type was fee-paying colleges with a science laboratory where students could study subjects like Chemistry, Physics and Biology. They had a very good reputation; however, their fees were very steep. Accordingly, only those students who could afford to pay such fees were able to attend these schools. My brother's friends who passed their School Certificate Examination and later become teachers attended such schools.

The third type was also fee-paying. However, they did not have a science laboratory, so any students attending such a school could not study Physics, Chemistry and Biology. They were in fact third tier colleges with a poor reputation for success. I had the misfortune of attending such a college, primarily because the fees were quite low compared to the second type of college. My brother equally attended such a school. Looking back, I often wonder whether his poor performance was due to the quality of the teaching he experienced. Although I knew the reputation of such schools, I had no other choice. The classes were overcrowded and, as the building was situated near a busy main road, the teachers were often drowned out by the noise of the traffic. However, I was determined to make the most of my opportunity.

In the beginning, I found it quite challenging to readapt to college life. Sitting all day on a hard bench and concentrating on what teachers were saying was quite taxing. I was not used to this kind of life. I thought labouring in the field was hard enough, as it sapped my physical energy. But assimilating knowledge and making sense of all the issues the teachers expected me to understand was mentally demanding and at the end of the day I was totally exhausted.

Form IV was divided into two distinct groups: A and B. Those who were studying in Group B were the re-sit group. They had failed their Form IV examination. Group A students had all passed their examination on their first sitting, and they were following a different syllabus. I was placed in Group A, which surprised me considering my background. But the Principal must have been influenced by my performance at the entrance test. Most of the students came from rural areas. Like me, they spoke Bhojpuri, and being able to communicate freely with them helped me adapt to the routine of school life. Many of them came from a similar background to mine, and at lunchtime we often shared experiences. Since I was ashamed of my work as a sugarcane labourer, I do not remember ever openly sharing the experiences of my time in the fields. It was too painful, and I felt that sharing with them would lower me in their estimations.

After six months, travelling to school on my bicycle came to an abrupt end. One morning I was running late for school and pedalling fast when I was involved in an accident with a taxi on a busy road in Port Louis. The taxi hit me side on and I was thrown in the middle of the road. Luckily the oncoming cars stopped in time and, apart from my bruised pride, I escaped practically unhurt. But my precious bicycle was severely damaged. The taxi driver was at fault, as he had failed to stop at the crossroads, but I did not pursue the case in the Mauritian Court as it was going to cost money to hire a lawyer and an attorney. Ma was horrified when she heard of the accident. She wanted me to travel by bus. But I knew that this was out of the question. I felt very sad to have lost my bicycle. I enjoyed that journey; it gave me precious time to reflect on what I had learned at school.

This accident caused a great stir in the family, and pricked the conscience of my sister and brother-in-law, Jannee and Moona. At that time my sister and her husband were living with his half-brother in one of the rooms of a three-bedroom house which was constructed mainly of iron sheeting. Attached to the house was a large kitchen. On the right of the kitchen there was long barn-like building in which there were six beds. This was where almost all the boys and their two male cousins slept. The cousins were boarders who were studying in one of the well-known fee-paying colleges. Despite the constraints of accommodation, my brother-in-law still invited me to come and live with him. He made an arrangement with his half-brother for me to sleep in the barn with the boys while attending my schooling in Port Louis. At the time I did not think twice about the consequences for Moona's family.

Chapter Eighteen

Ma was, at first, totally against the idea of me staying with my brother-in-law, who I addressed as Beau-Frère, as according to Hindu custom it is impolite to refer to one's brother-in-law by his first name. Ma did not want to be seen to be accepting charity. She thought it would show the world her plight; as being too poor to support her son's education. She insisted that I should go by bus, and said she would borrow money from a money lender to pay my bus fares. I knew that the money lenders were scroungers and she would become forever indebted to them. I did not want her to take any risk. Although I was reluctant to take up Moona's offer, I decided it was the only option.

'Ma, I want to stay with my brother-in-law. You do not have to be ashamed of our position in life. His sisters-in-law's brothers are staying there. It will be good for me to mix with these boys. They may be able to help me with my studies.'

In the end Ma half-heartedly accepted the arrangement. She told me that once a month she would send some money for my board and lodging. She made a condition with me that I had to return to the village every weekend. I do not remember ever receiving that promised sum.

Departing from Ma, my youngest sister, my brother and my village was not easy. I knew I was leaving behind the freedom of the countryside and my own home for the second time. In the village I knew practically everybody, and was well versed in village life. In the village environment and at home I spoke Bhojpuri,. In Port Louis and at the home of my brother-in-law everybody spoke Creole, a distorted version of the French language. Since I was not very fluent in Creole, I had great difficulty in adapting to the city life of Port Louis.

In the evening we all ate together. At home I ate all my meals with my fingers. We did not have spoons or metal plates. In the presence of the boys, I soon learnt that it was more civilised to eat with a spoon. I was told by the boys that only the lower castes ate their meals with their fingers. It was obvious they saw themselves belonging to the upper caste. It was not the first time I had been humiliated because of custom and practice in the village. Memories flashed by of Saint Paul, where I had been seen as a backward boy with no manners. I was still very naive about life generally and wanted to adapt quickly so that I could become one of them.

When I came back from school the house was always busy and raucous. I had no privacy. It was difficult to find a quiet place where I could do my homework. The radio was on more or less all the time. The boys had their own corners where they somehow managed to sit and study despite the incessant noise of Hindi songs emanating from the radio. I was not used to such noise. At home we never had a radio. The only noises that disturbed the peace of our village were those of cockerels and dogs. My new abode was suffocating me.

There were fifteen individuals, including myself, living in that house, with only one toilet: seven boys, three teenage girls and four adults. And they all knew their turn in the morning queue of using that toilet. On my second day in this new environment, without giving much thought to the pressing needs of others, I stayed in the toilet longer than they thought necessary. When I came out, five individuals including Moona's half-brother were waiting outside the toilet. They were all glaring at me. I knew I had broken the toileting rules.

'You must wait for your turn my son,' he said.

It was a difficult time for me. I knew I had to persevere with this arrangement if I was to make progress with my study. Determined to make the most of this opportunity, I decided to ignore any discomfort I suffered. My study became my only priority. My overall objective was to pass my examination and improve my standard of living and that of my family.

From day one, it was apparent, that I was not very welcome in the house. The boys remained aloof from me and hardly tried to engage me in any serious conversation. I was left to find my way by myself, probably, in the main, because of my shyness and difficulties with the language. After three months, I told my sister I was not very happy living in that environment. Without my knowledge, my brother-in-law had already started seeking alternative accommodation, and I was soon informed that in a week's time we were going to live at his father's place, which was only three houses away. Beau-Frère possessed his own land next to his father's house, but it was a barren place. His father owned a big house with four bedrooms and he gave one of the bedrooms to Moona. It was at this time I found out that my brother-in-law had a brother who occupied the other three bedrooms in the house. He was four years younger than Moona and was a married man with three children. There had been a rift between Moona and his father and real brother, because Moona had chosen to live with his half-brother following the re-marriage of his father after Moona's mother died. It was my mother, I found out later, who had played an active part in bringing father and son together and had managed to persuade Moona's father to help with accommodation.

Although my sister and brother-in-law were to occupy just one bedroom in that big house, they still wanted me to come and live with them.

'Where am I going to sleep?' I enquired.

'You will have your own room. Nobody is going to bother you anymore. Now you can study in peace.' He beamed with a great big smile on his face.

The next day, when he came from work, Moona took me to show me his father's house. I walked to the place with great anticipation. Their room was completely separate from the big house, and had a tiny cooking area outside with three large stones similar to those we had at home in the village. There was enough room for just one person in the cooking area, which was protected from the elements by three rusted iron sheets. There were two toilets in the yard. Both had running water and were connected to the main drainage system. One of them was solely for the use of the five tenants of his father. These tenants were living in tiny rooms in a long barn-like building that was made of corrugated iron sheets. The tenants had no kitchen of their own; they did all their cooking in the open air with pieces of wood between three bricks, like my sister in her tiny cooking area.

'Well, where is my room, Beau-Frère?' I asked.

'Here it is.'

Moona, pointed to the corridor adjacent to his bedroom. His eyes were shining with great excitement. There was a small wooden bed in the corridor and a table. There was no place for a chair, so I had to sit on the edge of the bed to study. There was an electric lamp hanging from the ceiling. He had made a small bookshelf at the side of the bed and on it stood a rusty winding clock that showed the correct time. I was pleased about the arrangement but mildly disappointed, as I thought that I was going to have a room of my own. But this den was a lot better than my previous accommodation at his half-brother's place. I hugged him with delight and thanked him.

I lived in that corridor for nearly two years. During that time, I had little contact with Moona's father or his younger brother. The only time I saw them was when they were using the facilities of the family toilet. Otherwise, they would lock themselves in the house, protected by the two guard dogs in their private yard.

At his half-brother's house, Beau-Frère had been able to listen to Indian songs. He would sit two metres from the radio nearly every evening when he came from work and hum to his favourite songs. I suppose that was his way of relaxing, although the sounds of the radio were a great source of irritation to me. One day, when I arrived home from college to my new accommodation, I heard the sound of a radio in his room. I stepped in the room and saw Beau-Frère sitting by a speaker, from which the sounds of Indian music were emanating.

'Oh, you have bought a new radio, Beau-Frère?'

'Oh no, this is not a radio. It is a speaker, Jaysingh. I have managed to persuade my father to connect his radio to this speaker. Every time they switch their radio on, we can listen to it at the same time.'

'How interesting,' I said with a flat tone in my voice. 'Can you turn it off at any time?'

'Oh, yes. You only have to remove this lead from the speaker.'

I would come home from college about four o'clock, about two hours before Beau-Frère. With the permission of my sister, I would disconnect the lead from the speaker, which gave me a peaceful and a quiet environment in which to complete my homework. I always ensured that before Beau-Frère's arrival the speaker was reconnected again. He was a hard worker and a dedicated husband, and I did not want to deprive him of his favourite pastime.

Beau-Frère hardly went anywhere in the evenings. On rare occasions he would visit his half-brother, and once he took us to the cinema when a film with his favourite actor was shown. On most evenings, for at least half an hour, he would spend time talking to me, and sometimes he would just sit by me while I was completing my homework.

One morning, as I was going to the family toilet, I heard the sound of footsteps on the gravel behind me.

'Hey, Jaysingh, why are you using this toilet? You are supposed to be using the other toilet.'

Moona's father was standing behind me. I looked at him, guiltily.

'Beau-Frère told me to use the family toilet, as we are the family of the house.'

'Yes, but you are not. You should use the tenants' toilet.'

I was very puzzled. Since Moona was my brother-in-law, I was surely part of the family. It was clear to me then that he saw me an outsider. I told my brother-in-law when he came home from work, which led to a bitter row between father and son. I regretted being the source of it. From then on, despite my brother-in-law's assurance that it was okay for me to use the family toilet, I decided to use the tenant's toilet to keep peace within the family.

While I was living in the corridor, Moona started to have his own house built. It took nearly a year to be completed. The new house comprised three bedrooms with a veranda and an attached kitchen. My sister and Beau-Frère at last had their own house. After a lavish puja we all moved to our new accommodation. I do not recall seeing his father there, but his two brothers and all their children were present. It was a memorable occasion. My sister and brother-in-law were delighted to have their own house.

At last, I had my own proper room with a door, comfortable bed, a writing table, a wooden chair and a glass cabinet with four bookshelves in it. I was eighteen years old by then and it was the first time I could honestly say that I was able to shut the bedroom door and the whole room was mine. I could now study in total privacy thanks to the efforts of my brother-in-law and sister.

The precious radio speaker, however, was not left behind, and was now connected by a ten-metre lead from his father's house.

One day I arrived home from college and could not hear the sound of the radio.

'Is the speaker broken, Didi?' I asked, puzzled.

'Oh, no; they have disconnected the speaker's lead from the radio. His brother gave no reasons for the disconnection. He only shouted over the fence that, since we have a new house, we can buy our own radio.'

When Beau-Frère arrived home, he was very displeased but refused to go and see his brother, despite much pleading by my sister. He remained very quiet all evening and hardly spoke to me. It was obvious he was upset. Next day when I arrived home from college, I was delighted to hear the sound of music coming, but this time from the veranda. It was only four o'clock, but my brother-in-law was already home, sitting in front of a brand-new radio, his face shining with amusement.

'Do you like our new radio?'

'Oh, yes. It looks beautiful, Beau-Frère.'

'Now we have our own radio. We do not have to rely on the charity of others. They have been good to us all this time. I suppose it was time we bought our own radio.'

Chapter Nineteen

Every day I walked to the college, which was half a mile away from my sister's house. Since I did not have any pocket money, I often ran back to her place for my lunch as I had done during my primary school days running home to share lunch with my Dadi. At other times I was hesitant to visit their house, and I just drank a bellyful of water at lunchtime while my college friends could afford to eat a whole sardine sandwich. I was very conscious that my brother-in-law was feeding me and giving me free accommodation. He also bought some schoolbooks for me. I made every effort not to make myself a source of irritation and disruption to their private lives. Although I was treated as one of the family, I could not forget that I was there because of their charity. So, I made a conscious effort to miss lunch at least twice a week and save them some money. Sometimes when my brother-in-law had a good day at work, he would give me pocket money. I would save this money to buy ink, pencils and paper. One lunchtime, unable to bear seeing my friends eating their sardine lunch, I decided to spend my twenty cents. So, I went to the shop salivating at the thought of eating sardines at last.

'Can I have a small bread roll with half a sardine in it, please?'

'Half a sardine? We don't sell half a sardine my boy,' he said loudly, and looked at me sympathetically.

I felt very embarrassed, as two of my classmates were just behind me.

‘I’m sorry. I meant one sardine. But it does not matter; I have left my money in the classroom.’

I found out later that a small roll and one sardine would have cost me thirty cents. In a way, I was glad that I came out of the shop empty-handed, as I’d managed to avoid revealing my financial situation to my friends.

For nearly a year I attended the school every day and performed quite well in all my subjects. My favourite subjects were Mathematics, British History and Latin. In fact, I was top of the class in History and from then on was a quite popular with Mr Pratap, the History teacher. I enjoyed being at school and studying with friends, and always completed my homework and ensured that the teacher saw my work and gave me feedback. I also participated in school sports, particularly football and running, and on the annual sports day I was beaten by ten yards in the three-mile race to come in second, and for that effort I received three rupees as a prize.

It was during my second year in Port Louis I noticed I was having problems seeing the writing on the blackboard. At that time, I was sitting at the back of the class. When I mentioned my dilemma to the teacher, he made a special arrangement for me to sit on the first bench. My new position in the class did improve my ability to see the board for a while, but sadly my eyesight later deteriorated to such an extent that I had to mention it to my brother-in-law. I knew all along that my mother did not have the money to buy me reading glasses and was very hesitant to mention it to my benefactors.

‘Silly, Jaysingh,’ said Beau-frère, ‘why didn’t you mention this to me before?’

Next day he took me to an optician, and within four weeks I received a pair of white-framed reading glasses. I never found out how much my generous brother-in-law paid for my eye test and glasses.

At the beginning of my stay in Port Louis, I would go home to my village nearly every week. I would leave Port Louis Friday afternoon and return to the city Monday morning. Somehow, my mother managed to find my bus fares. I would miss my family very much when I returned to Port Louis, particularly my younger sister, Deomatee. Before I left home, Deomatee and I had established a beautiful brother and sister bond. When I was working as a labourer, I would always buy something for her, like jelly babies on my pay day. She would prepare my food parcel and hand it to me as I left for work with a great big smile on her face. In the evenings I would often play hopscotch with her and two girls who lived opposite our house. I missed all that sisterly love in Port Louis.

Overall, I do not have happy memories of my weekend visits. The poverty at home was quite bad. My brother had still not found a settled job. He tried working in the local village shop, but that did not last long. He felt working as a salesman was worse than working in the field. At least in the field he could hide himself from the glare of the villagers. But in the shop, everybody could see how far he had fallen from the dizzy height of being a school teacher. The presence of his close friends, who were now working as teachers, was an added humiliation. In a desperate attempt to find employment for him away from the village, Ma found a clerical job for him in Port Louis in a well-established shop, Tulsidas, which sold garments for ladies and gentlemen. The owner was one of Ma's distant cousins. Even this job did not last long. He had a bitter quarrel with the owner one day, because he was accused of being a zombie. In the end the only place for him was to work on our land, which by then was barren.

The pitiful and sad atmosphere at home in the village affected me a lot. Instead of studying I would roam about in the nearby fields wondering how I was going to improve the life of the family. I did not have any privacy and could not concentrate on my homework. Besides, I could not carry all my books with me during my weekend stay, as I had to leave behind the heavy Mathematics book. It became apparent to me that weekend visits were disrupting my study. I was in a great dilemma, as if I stayed seven days a week in Port Louis it would cost my adopted family far more than initially agreed. In the end I decided my study should come first, and started visiting my village home every third weekend. My brother-in-law did not mind. In fact, he was pleased in some respects. During the weekend, when my homework was finished, we would walk around the mountains that line the boundaries of Port Louis. It was great fun being with him.

One Sunday morning Beau-frère was in a good mood.

'Jaysingh, get ready we are going to climb the mountain to-day!'

'But Beau-frère I have heard there are big monkeys there. They are not very friendly animals.'

'Oh, don't be a coward. Forget your study for to-day. Let us relax and enjoy the views from the top of the mountain.'

Didi was equally excited. She handed us our sandwiches and bottles of water.

'Off you go. But be careful there.'

Well, what a memorable day it was. Beau-frère and I like two friends spent nearly four hours together. We stood on top of the mountain and admired the panoramic view of Port-Louis and the harbour. We ate wild apples and chased the monkeys. He tried to enliven my life when I was drowning under the weight of my personal troubles.

Chapter Twenty

At the beginning of my third year at the college it became apparent Ma had not been able to keep up the payment of school fees, as the milking cow had suddenly gone dry, and my brother was unable to obtain a paid job.

One morning the school administrator called me into his office and told me Ma had not paid the fees for three months and if all the arrears were not paid within a month, I would be asked to stop attending the school. The news shocked me. I felt my internal organs shaking within my body and could hardly concentrate on my studies during class.

'What's wrong, Jaysingh?' the boy sitting next to me asked when I returned from the Principal's office. 'You seem to be in a different world.'

'I am rather anguished Ram. I just heard some bad news, and I am trying to figure out what is the best way to deal with it.'

I wanted to tell him of my plight, but we were interrupted by the Principal who was due to start his English Literature class. He glanced at me, and I knew what his eyes were saying: You should not be in this class. You have not paid the school fees. I knew very well the circumstances of Ma. She was saving money for my younger sister's wedding dowry, and was paying a hundred rupees every month towards the cost of the one acre of land she had bought near Trou Aux Biches at the beginning of my first year at college. While the Principal was explaining the plot of *Silas Marner*, I was thinking of the day when Ma bought that land from Dr Jhubboo, a very rich

French landlord who owned most of the land by the sea. Ma took me to his office in Trou aux Biches. He was sitting on his leather chair, wearing dark rimmed glasses. Two Creole male servants were standing in the room. When we walked in his office, after a wait of nearly two hours, he looked closely at me and at Ma, who was wearing a tattered red sari. Her hair was all in knots and roughly tied on top of her head in a seashell-shaped style.

'Well, you have seen the land that you want to buy. Now tell me how you intend to pay for it?' he said in broken French so that Ma could understand him.

'Master, I'm a very poor lady, but I want a piece of land for my children. If you agree, I'll pay 200 rupees every month without fail until the full amount of 5000 rupees is paid.'

He looked at Ma again, this time without his glasses, then called his legal adviser and asked him to draw a contract which stated that *'Miss Indranee Servansing has agreed hereafter to pay 100 rupees monthly for the purchase of the aforesaid land. In case of any default of payment she should be given every opportunity to pay the rest without any added interest.'* Ma was addressed as Miss Indranee Servansingh because she was not civilly married.

He asked the adviser, who could speak Bhojpuri, to explain the terms of the contract to Ma. When she understood the terms, Ma rushed to Dr Jhubboo and touched his feet with great reverence.

'No, Indranee, you go home. If you have any problems in your payment, you come and see me.'

When we left his office, Ma was elated. ‘I own that land. What a generous man, what a kind man,’ she kept saying. ‘Remember, Jaysingh, if you are honest to people any problems can be resolved.’

Because of his kindness, Ma maintained the monthly payment without fail, even when that meant sacrificing my school fees. I wondered many times during my second year whether Ma had financial difficulties, as she sometimes could not find enough money to pay for my bus fares during my weekend visits. Honestly, I do not think she realised the consequence of non-payment of the school fees. She had promised the French landlord, and it was crucial for her pride not to default on any payments.

One Monday morning, when we were all lined up for the usual college assembly, I heard my name shouted out by the Principal.

‘Woogara, you come here’.

I walked up the ten concrete steps under the piercing gaze of my fellow students and the teachers, all the time wondering what I had done to deserve such attention. While climbing the steps I was convinced that I was due to be honoured for the top marks I had received in History and Mathematics the week before. So I was quite shocked when I heard the angry tone of the Principal.

‘Woogara, you have not paid your school fees for six months. You have been warned several times. I have no choice but to ask you to leave the school now,’ he said, pointing to the metal gate.

I was stunned and devastated at being thrown out of the school in such a humiliating manner. To be degraded in front of a teacher in privacy was bearable, but to be treated like a criminal in front of all my fellow students in such an undignified way was very difficult to swallow.

In front of nearly three hundred students and with tears running down my cheeks, I was forced to march out of the college. I cursed and blamed myself for not telling Ma and Beau-frère when the school administrator had warned me. I could have sought help from my brother-in-law. But I kept it to myself thinking that the Principal, being a pleasant and honest looking man, would not dare throw me out of his school when I was progressing so well in all my subjects. I had explained to the administrator many times that quite probably Ma was having difficulty in finding the money. But to the Principal, running the school was a business. I could not blame him. I swallowed my pride and walked out with a bowed head.

I did not know what to do when I was outside the school. I could have gone to my sister and poured it all out to her, but instead I chose to keep my humiliation quiet. I spent that day in the Port-Louis public library wondering what would happen to my life and my future now that the dream of school days was shattered.

Despite the fact that I was thrown out of the school in an inhumane manner, I persisted going three more days. Every time the Principal refused to have me back. Having been belittled in front of the school assembly for the fourth time, my future looked very bleak. I was too ashamed to mention my plight to anybody, particularly Ma. I even kept the secret from my sister and Beau-frère. I hatched a plan. Every day, instead of going to the college, I started spending the school hours in the public library. I created for myself a rigid timetable and stuck to it and thus ensured that I studied all the subjects.

The public library was well stocked with schoolbooks. I knew that I was not able to take the Cambridge School Certificate Examination as I had to be studying full time as a student at a college. My only solution was to study for the GCE Ordinary Level (O level) examination, as at that time any student could take that examination as a private pupil. I studied the O Level syllabus in detail and had a pretty good idea what I was expected to cover to meet the syllabus requirements.

Once a week I would cycle to a friend's house who lived two miles from Port Louis. We used to sit together during my school days, so he knew my financial difficulties. We both belonged to the same Hindu caste and that cemented our friendship. We spent at least three hours every Saturday morning discussing the work he had been doing at school. If I had any difficulties with mathematical problems or any other challenging questions, I would discuss them with him. With his help I maintained the momentum of my study. It was a miracle that during this time none of my family discovered my difficult position.

One day the library clerk, who had seen me attending the library every day, called me to his desk.

'What is your name?'

I could not lie because he could have found out my name as I was a member of the library.

'Why aren't you at school?'

I could not tell him the truth, so I informed him I liked this private mode of studying. I think he must have sussed out my financial difficulties and from then on allowed me access to the library before the opening time of nine o'clock and looked after my belongings when I went to my sister's house for lunch.

On Monday mornings, for nearly eight weeks, I continued turning up at school, knowing full well the consequence. I naively thought the Principal would feel sorry for me, and allow me to attend the school despite my financial difficulties. After two months of such persistent actions, I was informed by the school administrator that the Principal wanted to see me in his office.

'Woogara, you know very well that you haven't paid the school fees for six months. Why do you keep coming to the school? You know the school policy.'

'Yes Sir. I want to study, but Ma has no money to pay the school fees.'

I told him about my free board and lodging at my sister's place and that there was no way I could ask her to pay my school fees. I also explained to him how I had been studying in the public library every day without the knowledge of my family. When I showed him my study timetable, I could detect the sudden change in his expression.

'Woogara, I'm very impressed by your determination but you do need a lot of help. I want you to come to my house this Friday evening at six o'clock.'

He ushered me out without any further explanation. That Friday evening, I ensured I would arrive at the Principal's place on time. I got to his house at half past five. He was already giving private lessons to a group of five students. His wife asked me to wait in the lounge. Around quarter past six I was shown into the dining room. The Principal was eating on his own at a round wooden table. He asked me to sit by him. I hesitated. It was too informal for me. I had always seen the Principal in his best suit, and here he was sitting and eating curry and rice with his fingers.

'Woogara, have you had your evening meal?'

'No Sir. But I was going to have my meal after my meeting with you.'

'Roshni?'

'Yes, Prem.'

'Bring some food for Woogara. He is starving.'

'But, Sir!'

'You eat first, and then I am going to talk to you.'

I did not know what to make out of the scenario. I was flabbergasted that he was feeding me. I knew I was malnourished, because the clerk of the library had remarked about it many times. But here was the man who had thrown me out of his school, had belittled and humiliated me several times in front of at least 300 students, and now was treating me as if I were his son. I could only thank my Karma. I slowly ate the curry and rice with my right hand but did not enjoy it.

After the meal we washed our hands with soap and water and made our way to his study. The place was lined with bookshelves full of books standing upright like soldiers. The room was quite big, at least twice as big as my bedroom. There were three sofas and a long mahogany table with eight brown chairs. We sat on the sofas and he explained how he was planning to help me for a while. He questioned me about the books I had been reading and how I was coping with my mathematics. In the end he agreed to help me with my study. When I left his house, my confidence surged. At last, I felt I had some sort of future.

From that day onwards my life changed for the better. Every Friday, for nearly nine months, I made that short journey to the Principal's place and he tutored me, free of charge, in English Literature, English and French. He also arranged for one of his teachers to help me with Latin each Wednesday.

At the end of that year, I took my O Level examination privately and obtained passes in Mathematics, Latin and British History. I received a borderline failure grade in English, French and English Literature. It was a miracle I managed to obtain passes in three subjects when the Principal had advised me I was not yet ready to take the examination. But, at that time, I was very confident in my ability.

I was proud of my achievement. And although I had passed only three subjects, I was not too downhearted, because

I had failed the other three subjects by five marks only. I knew if I took the O level examination a second time, I would be successful. But the question that nagged at me was how I was to pay my examination fees for the second time? I knew Ma could not spare the lofty sum of one hundred rupees. But I had to find that sum within four months if I was to take my re-sit examination at the next attempt in June 1966. The problem seemed insurmountable.

One day I was in a bookshop perusing an English Literature book when somebody gently tapped on my shoulder. It was a policy of the shop that the pages of any books should not be opened. I had been flouting this policy on many occasions and thought it was the bookshop manager who had at last caught me in the act. But to my amazement and delight it was my school History teacher, Mr Pratap.

'Hello, Woogara. How are you? I am very sorry about the way you have been treated at the school. Are you attending another school?'

'No Sir.'

'Come along for a cup of coffee with me, and you can tell me all about yourself. You know, Woogara, I have been wondering about you for a while, and here you are. You were one of my best pupils.'

Mr Pratap took me to a very special coffee shop that only tourists and wealthy Mauritians frequented. He ordered two pieces of cake and two cups of coffee. To tell the truth, it was the first time in my life I had been served by a uniformed waiter and tasted coffee. Most of the customers were white.

They were immaculately dressed and seemed to me engaged in serious conversation. There were a few Mauritians who did not pay much attention to us, but the white customers kept peering at us, which made me uncomfortable for a while. Mr Pratap realised my feeling and told me not to pay any attention to them.

Without hesitation, I told Mr Pratap my plight and my private study pattern in the public library and how the Principal was helping me towards my O Level examination. When we left the coffee shop, he put twenty rupees in my hand and asked me to come and meet him in the café in five days' time. At first, I refused to take the money, but at his insistence accepted it. The shiny coins were appealing; I knew in my heart I wanted them desperately.

When I visited that luxurious café on the second occasion, Mr Pratap was sitting in the lounge reading a newspaper. He greeted me with great delight.

'I have got a surprise for you. I have found you a job. You have been accepted to teach Latin and Mathematics at Dayananad Anglo-Vedic College at a salary of seventy-five rupees (about £2) a month.'

I sat there dumbfounded. I thought I was dreaming. I asked him to repeat what he'd said.

'Don't I have to be interviewed, Sir?'

'Oh, don't worry about that. The Principal is my friend. You are starting on Monday. You need a tie and a long-sleeved white shirt.'

On our way out, he shook my hand, handed me an envelope and told me I was to meet him on the first Monday of every month in the bookshop where we'd first met. He did not linger around for me to thank him, leaving the scene at full gallop. It took me five minutes to fully comprehend my situation. I tried to run after Mr Pratap, but he had vanished among the crowds, and I had no idea where he lived. I leaned against a lamppost and opened the envelope. In it was an introductory letter to give to the Principal of the college and the sum of fifty rupees.

I wanted to run up and down the road and shout to the world that I was a teacher.

'Oh, Almighty Hanumanji, how am I to thank you for what you have done for me.'

After much deep thought I was still not quite sure who my best benefactor was. I ran to my brother-in-law's workshop, told him about the events of the day and showed him the fifty rupees Mr Pratap had given me.

It was Friday, and I needed a tie and a shirt. That afternoon Beau-frère took me to a men's garment shop and bought them for me. I had to try them on several times before he was satisfied of their suitability. It was the first time I had ever worn long trousers and a long-sleeved shirt. I was very happy, a feeling that cannot be described clearly in words. As my Dadi had told me, 'The revolving sun will one day shine its light on you'. I just hoped and prayed that those wretched shadows would stay away.

My visit to my village home that weekend was very different from the previous visits. I thought I was walking on air. When Ma heard the news, she hugged me. Tears streamed down her cheeks. Instead of rejoicing, she was loudly sobbing. That night, when I lay on my dry sugarcane thatched bed, I could not help remembering the other advice that Dadi gave me: 'If you work hard enough, my sona, you will achieve your dream.'

Chapter Twenty-One

During the middle of 1964 while I was spending my time in the public library because I had been thrown out of school, important events were developing in my village home.

One November Sunday, when I was at home for the weekend, my youngest sister, Deomatee, now fifteen years old, was preparing to be introduced to a possible suitor, as part of an arranged marriage. My brother-in-law, sister and one of Ma's male cousins from Port Louis were all present. Since all our rattan chairs had holes in them, we had borrowed good quality chairs from our neighbours for everyone to sit on. The prospective suitor was a young man, Bissoon, who was the fifth son of the Judoo family. The Judoo brothers were well known in Mauritius at that time. They were very wealthy and owned a huge garment factory in Rose Hill that specialised in making quality shirts. They also had many shops in various towns. I had been window-shopping at one of their shops in Port Louis and was very impressed by the display of shirts. I'd wanted to step inside and try on a shirt, but I knew they were beyond my means. Their shirts were fashionable, and it was a young man's dream to wear Judoo Fils shirts.

My sister was very nervous as the appointed time of two o'clock approached. I told Ma that Deomatee was too young to enter into an arranged marriage. She was only fifteen years old and had no idea about life generally. But I was hushed.

'It is a great match. She is going to a rich family.'

'But she is too young, Ma, and I understand from Beau-frère that he is at least ten years older than her.'

'Don't worry, Jaysingh. Age does not matter. She will grow up. Besides, there is no point in her staying here in this poor household. She will never have such an opportunity again. She will be a rich lady with many servants. She is a very fortunate girl. It's her Karma, her Karma, Jaysingh.'

Well, my future brother-in-law and his relatives were not shy in showing their wealth, arriving in two Mercedes and a BMW. I doubt whether our villagers had ever seen such cars in the neighbourhood. Since the road was rather narrow, with no parking spaces outside our place, the cars had to be parked in the neighbours' yards. Despite the intense summer heat, all five brothers were dressed identically, in blue suits, ties and white, pointed leather shoes. The four ladies were equally immaculately dressed in beautiful pink saris with golden necklaces and bracelets. I was very impressed by their appearance and told my sister so.

'Bhaya, let us pray that none of them will be seeking to meet the call of nature. What are we going to do? I have told Ma to have a latrine built. We cannot tell them to use the sugarcane fields.'

'Don't worry, Dev. Of course, I'll show them the sugarcane fields. After all, that's where we go.'

She laughed and gently pushed me aside. I was happy, but equally I felt sad at the prospect of my sister marrying and leaving the village home. She was so innocent, but very beautiful, with big brown eyes and long flowing hair. And whereas I was rather dark, my sister had very fair skin. I could see she was nervous, as she kept holding my hand tightly. One of the ladies helped Deomatee into a red sari and gold necklace that Ma had borrowed from one of her relatives. She looked more beautiful than ever. I thought Bissoon would be a fool to refuse her.

Following the introduction of my sister to the group, and the subsequent discussion with Ma and my brother-in-law, it became apparent the family liked the appearance and manners of my sister. Despite my reservation about Bissoon being ten years older than my sister, I was delighted with the match. Deomatee was an intelligent girl. After all, she was educated up to sixth standard and was well versed in Hindi. Most importantly for the Judoo family, she was a village girl.

At that time city girls were frowned upon by the rich Hindu families. They were seen to have too much freedom and to have lost the ability to show respect to the Elders. The city girls were seen to be argumentative, as they sought parity with men. Whereas the village girls were viewed as less sophisticated; and the Judoo family wanted their wives to be subservient to their husbands. So, the family approved the match, and it was agreed that after six months of supervised courtship the wedding would take place in May of 1965.

When Ma was looking for a prospective husband for Deomatee, without my knowledge she had also been on the lookout for a wife for my brother. She was concerned that following the marriage of my sister there would be nobody at home to do the domestic chores while she was away in the fields. She equally and reasonably decided that if both of them could marry on the same day a good portion of money could be saved. For a Hindu wedding a marquee had to be built and at least a hundred guests had to be invited and fed for nearly two days. Beau-frère had endorsed her plan, and once my sister's wedding was fixed the search for a bride for my brother started in earnest.

By this time my brother had a steady job as a road builder supervisor. He was employed by the local council and so the job was quite secure. He had reached the age of twenty-four and Ma thought that it was time he should be tied down with a partner. The government was investing large sums of money in the building of side roads like ours, and he was part of this project. It was a poorly paid job, but at least he was no longer unemployed. Besides this job, he was also helping Ma work our land, particularly with the planting of sugarcane, maize and peanuts. It was obvious he was able to support a wife, so the search was in full swing.

After two unsuccessful attempts they found a family that was agreeable to a marriage between their daughter, Neera, and my brother. Her father was not fussy about the status of my brother's job. According to Neera, her father was mainly concerned that my brother came from the Chhetri caste and that she was not going to be starved. Neera was a village girl from the north of Mauritius and, just like my own sister, was only fifteen years old when the match was accepted. My brother liked her because she had very fair skin. He did not mind that she was only educated up to third standard of primary school and was not literate in either the Hindi or English languages. But she was a fluent speaker of Creole. I only found out about his impending wedding when, one weekend I was visiting, my brother asked me whether I wanted to stay in Port Louis.

'Why are you asking me such a question?'

'Well, you know, I'll be getting married soon, and as our house is small, I thought you would like to stay in Port Louis.

'Oh no. When I pass my O Level I should like to stay here permanently. I am fed up with moving about from one place to another. I shall obtain a job in the government and live near you. Won't it be great for two brothers to live side by side? Do you remember, that's what our Dadi wanted?'

He gave the impression he was not pleased with my answer.

Before the wedding Ma ensured that a proper latrine was built at the back of the house. She did not want her guests to use the sugarcane fields, as the owners had started complaining about the filthy state of their land. A relative of ours made a concrete seat with a rectangular hole in the middle. My brother and I dug a ten-foot-deep trench in the ground, supported the concrete seat on four wooden poles crossing the trench, and built a thatched hut around it. There was no running water or sink to wash one's hands. When nature called, one had to squat on top of the hole and wash one's bottom with water from a bottle by rubbing gently with the left fingers. That is why some Asians believe that the left hand is a dirty hand, and most Indians like eating their food with their right hand.

By the time the wedding day came the latrine was very smelly and attracting flies, which constantly buzzed around it. We sprinkled a large amount of salt into the pit to soak up the slimy waste, as it was practically full to the brim. I was used to the proper toilets we had in Port Louis. I felt sick when I used our latrine and was ashamed at the state of it. Unfortunately, a pit latrine was the best Ma could afford. At least it was preferable to running to the sugarcane fields. It was less anxiety producing, as we did not have to be on the lookout for the landowner in case we got caught on the job.

Ma had also built a fairly large brick kitchen adjoining the house. Before that we did not have a proper kitchen. Most of our cooking took place outdoors. Perhaps it was a requirement of Neera's father that his daughter have a decent kitchen. The new kitchen had a sink, running water, a gasoline stove and various storage cupboards. In short, it was quite a modern kitchen.

As Ma had hoped, my sister and brother were both having their wedding on the same day, which would save Ma money. But it was still going to be an expensive business. Some sort of dowry had to be given for my sister, and two pundits had to be paid to oversee the ceremony. My brother-in-law was in charge of planning the weddings, and I thought he did a good job. My brother's wedding took place in the morning and my sister's in the afternoon. All guests were fed around midday and they departed happily with a bag of wedding sweets in their hands. Ma had had to borrow a good sum of money to finance the event, but she was happy that three of her children were now married. I knew her financial difficulties and was not going to nag her to borrow more money to pay for my school fees.

In many ways I was excited I had a sister-in-law. We got on fairly well despite our shyness. But, although she was nearly three years younger than me, I still could not call her by her first name, as it would have been seen as very disrespectful. I had to address her as Bhowjee, which means sister-in-law.

Bhowjee's presence made a few changes in the house. She had brought a radio with her, a wedding gift from her father. It was rather strange to listen to the latest Hindi songs in our home. Ma was pleased, particularly as religious songs were broadcast at three o'clock every afternoon. She would sit down in the yard and listen to those songs with her eyes shut. Having the radio made us feel proud, because none of the neighbours had one in their house at that time. Although the radio was battery powered, Ma was conscious that the batteries would run down, and it distressed her when it was on for longer than necessary. Accordingly, after the initial period of showbiz, the radio remained mostly silent in the evening, with Bhowjee not wanting to upset Ma. The music and songs had also started annoying me during my weekend visits, but I remained quiet because, I soon realised, I did not have much say in the running of the house. I had become a stranger in my own home. It was difficult to study when the radio was on. Since the house was constructed with iron sheets at that time, and the doors were generally kept open because of the intense heat, it was difficult to contain the incessant sound of the radio. And, as my brother enjoyed listening to it, it did create tension between us. As time went on, I started coming to my village home less frequently. I felt there was nothing there for me to come home to. The atmosphere had completely changed. The serenity of my home had vanished and the chattering of my sister Dev was not there to welcome me. I felt awkward in the presence of Bhowjee as I did not know how to behave in front of her. She always tried her best to welcome me but my shyness hampered our relationship.

Two months after Deomatee's wedding I started missing her quite badly. I was always very attached to her and was yearning to find out how she was settling down in her new environment with the rich Judoo family. One Sunday, without the knowledge of Ma and my brother-in-law, I travelled by bus with three oranges in a white plastic bag to pay her a visit. I was in khaki shorts, a short-sleeved shirt and my rather dirty school plimsolls. When I arrived at the door of the four-bedroom house, I was greeted by the youngest Judoo brother. He informed me that they were having a business meeting and my sister could be found in the kitchen.

Deomatee was indeed in the kitchen, surrounded by hundreds of unwashed dishes, dirty pans and half-eaten curries. She was busy doing the washing-up and there was nobody to help her. Deomatee was delighted to see me. She hugged me and tears ran down her cheeks. She told me she was having difficulty adjusting to life within a large family. She shared the house with her mother-in-law and Bissoon's sister, and was expected to do all the cooking and washing-up. The other brothers frequented the house regularly with their wives and children and it was common practice to feed them. I was quite surprised to hear the other wives rarely stayed behind to help with the washing-up and there were no servants to assist her. It hurt me to see her plight. I could sense my sister was being used as a maid of the house, and had the impression the rich Judoo family had practically bought my sister because a poor village girl was less likely to complain. I never mentioned this to Ma. I knew it would have upset her. I mentioned it to Didi Janee and my brother-in-law, but I doubted they could do anything to help my dear sister. She had no choice but to adapt to the environment she was thrust in. She had to learn to cook for a large family with alien dishes. They enjoyed eating meat whereas we were mainly vegetarians.

Chapter Twenty-Two

When I started my teaching career in the February of 1966 at Dayananad Anglo-Vedic College, I was under the impression it was a full-time post. But on my first day I was told I was employed for only three days a week. It suited me fairly well because it gave me time to prepare for my re-sit O Level examination in June of that year. The entrance examination fees were due to be paid in the first week of March and, according to my calculation, I would by then have saved the required amount. It meant I did not have to beg money from anybody. Pride radiated from my eyes in brilliant flashes because I was then able to fund myself. I felt that was a great achievement in itself. I was very confident I would successfully achieve passes in the requisite five subjects in one sitting.

My plan was that once I had passed my O Level, I would aim for the Advanced Level examination. I knew I would have to attend a fee-paying school for a minimum period of two years and would need to carry on teaching for one full year to save enough money for the fees. The reward of success at Advanced Level was unimaginable. I knew a friend of my brother's had obtained a post as a civil servant in a government department following his success at A Level, and I often dreamt of obtaining employment as a civil servant like him or as a clerk in a bank. Both posts were seen as prestigious and well paid. Being a primary school teacher was prestigious enough, but I wanted more than that. There were already three primary school teachers in the village, but we had no civil servants or bank clerks.

On my first day at the College, I got up very early. I knew that the Port Louis Hindu temple usually opened its gates at six. Following a quick shower, I ran there with a bunch of flowers and thanked Hanumanji for shining some good fortune on me.

My sister and Beau-frère were equally excited. I felt like a different person when I had donned the long trousers, red tie and white long-sleeved shirt.

'You look like a real gentleman, Jaysingh,' my brother-in-law shouted from the kitchen. He was wearing a broad smile and I knew he was as proud as I was.

My sister kissed my cheeks and blessed me with some Hindu religious verses. 'Well done, Jaysingh and let us hope God will always support you.'

When I walked through the entrance of the college for the first time and saw the students playing in the yard, panic suddenly hit me. My legs felt like a jelly. All the confidence built up over the last few days suddenly evaporated. I just stood there as if suspended in mid-air. Gradually I came to earth and realised my position. I looked around and what struck me most on that first day was the realisation that those students that I recognised from Triolet were Aryan Hindus who believed Gods represented the forces of nature, and thought worshiping deity icons, as my family did, was morally and spiritually unacceptable. I was determined from that day that I would not divulge my Chhetri caste to anybody. Mr

Pratap knew my caste, and I thought he had communicated this to the Principal, who received me well and told me the key mission of the school was to improve the educational standards of the Aryans in Mauritius. I vehemently disapproved of this Aryan philosophy but very wisely kept my thoughts to myself. I soon concluded that he thought I belonged to the Aryan caste, because he openly criticised the Chhetri and Brahmin castes at staff meetings. His main argument was that although the upper caste was a minority group, they mostly occupied the top posts due to nepotism and favouritism from politicians. As I had been introduced by Mr Pratap, the Principal did not enquire about my caste background, and I did not volunteer the information.

For three months I was very happy at the college teaching Latin and Mathematics to Form 1 students. There were forty pupils in the class, all of them around the age of thirteen. They were mostly polite and addressed me as 'Sir'. Although I possessed only three O Levels, I thought I was quite competent in my subjects and had no difficulty in coping with the teaching load. In fact, after only two weeks, five students wanted me to give them private lessons, and they were willing to pay me ten rupees per month. I thought that overnight I had become a rich man, earning seventy rupees from the college and another fifty rupees from private tuition. My sister and brother-in-law were delighted by my change of fortune. At the end of each month, I even volunteered to give my sister twenty rupees for my upkeep but she refused to take them. It was a great feeling; at last, I was becoming financially independent.

Despite my elevated status, I continued with my study pattern in the public library on the remaining two days. I no longer ran to my sister's house for lunch. Instead, I was now able to buy my own luncheon in the market and even a cup of tea. I enjoyed eating sardine sandwiches more than any other food. I had imagined that those days spent salivating at the thought of eating such a delicacy were gone forever. The Principal of the High School continued giving me free lessons in the evening as if nothing had changed. He even fed me as before, despite the fact that he had full knowledge of my change of fortune. He refused to accept any tuition fees. In fact, he became very angry the day I offered him one month's fees.

'You keep it, Woogara. You need it more than me.'

After three months, my fortune suddenly took a dramatic change for the worse. It was the first day of May, and during my Latin period I was told to urgently report to the Principal. The Principal was sitting in a morose state when I reached his office. He did not respond to my greeting. I could see that his cheeks were quivering with anger. It was quite common for students to make complaints against teachers, and I thought, having observed his demeanour that this must be the case.

'Woogara, you did not tell me that you belonged to the Chhetri caste?'

I suddenly felt certain that an arrow had darted to my chest, paralysing my whole body with such an acute pain.

'You never asked me, sir. Besides, I thought Mr Pratap would have informed you of my caste.'

'No, he did not.'

'Do you think belonging to the Chhteri caste has affected my teaching?

He did not answer my question and I waited for the bombshell to drop.

'I am very sorry, Woogara. You have deceived me, and I want you to leave the college at once. I cannot keep a fraudster at my college. Although it is only first day of the month you will be paid the full monthly amount.'

'But sir, I did not deliberately deceive you. I am a good teacher. It is unfair that you, an educated man, should dismiss a teacher on the grounds of his caste.'

'The philosophy of the college is very clear, Woogara, and I am afraid you have violated it. From now on you are not welcome in the college.'

It was useless arguing with him. He had already decided I did not belong there. I staggered out of his office. For the second time my Chhetri caste bedevilled my life. I picked up my satchel, and without saying goodbye to my students, I marched out of the college with my head high, determined to prove to him one day that his philosophy of life and the principle on which he based his teaching was totally wrong. I had a great difficulty in comprehending the extent to which even so-called well-educated men had such a distorted view of the Hindu caste system.

I was so ashamed of this episode; I decided not to tell anybody the true reason for my dismissal from the college. In fact, I kept a positive front. I told them that teaching was taking too much of my time from my preparation for my O Level examination and left it to the family to reach any conclusion they thought fit. Ma and my brother thought it was madness on my part to leave a teaching career. Even my brother-in-law was disappointed. I still had the five private students, and I continued teaching them, although the venue changed to my brother-in-law's veranda.

Despite his disappointment my brother-in-law continued boarding me at his house. By this time, I had a nephew, Mahen, who was four years old and a demanding three-year-old niece, Madvi. I loved having them around. In the evening, while my sister was preparing the meal, I kept them occupied with games and reading. The children had developed a great affinity to me and wanted me to spend more and more of my time with them. This meant I could not focus on my own study until they had gone to bed. Very often Madvi sat on my lap in the evening while I was studying. To keep the two children quiet, I developed a strategy of reading Shakespeare's Macbeth to them. I simplified the story and it worked most of the time. All three of us benefited from this. I was revising and most importantly it kept the children interested in the play. I would routinely get up at four in the morning when the house was quiet and a lot cooler. It was at this time of the morning that I did most of my studying.

Following my dismissal from the college, I hardly went home to Triolet. I had started to see myself as a stranger in the very house I was born. The atmosphere was not very welcoming. Although, I was always delighted to see Ma, my brother and my sister-in-law, there was not the same closeness that I enjoyed with my sister and brother-in-law in Port Louis. By then I had been living there for nearly four years and had become truly part of the family. In the village home Ma was no longer in charge of running the house. She had become a bystander. She had started slowing down physically. There were no cows in the shed, and only two goats to keep her busy. I did miss Ma while I was in Port Louis, but I didn't miss my brother and sister-in-law very much. I was still a shy young man and I felt awkward in the village home. And although there was a latrine, I still had to have my bath in the backyard. Besides, I had changed. Staying at Port Louis had given me a different perspective on life. I had become an independent person in many respects. I was no longer the Jaysingh who cut sugarcane and played with Bhardoj, and now hardly saw my childhood friend during visits to my village home.

Chapter Twenty-Three

I had decided to take the same five subjects for my re-sit O Level examination as I had taken before: Pure Mathematics, Latin, British History, English Language and English Literature. My study became very intensive, and in order to spend more time in the library I started having my lunch in the market even though I had stopped working at the college. Mr Pratap continued his donation of ten rupees every month, and with the money I was receiving from tuition fees I had sufficient money at least to buy my own lunch.

My life dramatically changed by sheer coincidence one May morning in 1966. As was my custom, in between my subject studies, I was scanning the pages of a popular Mauritian daily newspaper in the public library, when my eyes fell on a small headline on the fourth page: *Student nurses required in UK. You are eligible to take the entrance examination if you have any three GCE Ordinary Levels.*

By then I was twenty years old and was still leading the pretence of being a college student and was wholly reliant on the goodness of my brother-in-law to lodge and feed me. At the beginning of that very month, I had been dismissed from my teaching position at the college. My ambition of completing my Advanced Level study had been totally dashed when both of my brothers-in-law had refused to support me financially. I had thought that since my younger brother-in-law, Bissoon, came from a rich family he would be willing to help me and had gone to see him.

'Bissoon, you are from such a rich family. Surely you can help your poor brother-in-law. I need financial help desperately to study at GCE Advanced Level. Once I have passed the examination and obtained a decent job, I assure you I will reimburse every penny that I borrow.'

'But Jaysingh, we are a Company. I do not get a salary or monthly bonuses. All my food and clothing are bought by the Company. Individually I do not have any savings. In fact, Moona is richer than I am in many respects. You have to understand, I am not against your study. I am just not able to help you financially.'

At that time my future looked bleak and empty. At times I was very depressed. I had already lost faith in my Hindu Gods and that there was no point running to the temple because nobody was listening to my pleading. It is true I had become suicidal. My only hope was to pass the O Level examination, and there was no certainty I would succeed.

When I scrutinised the small advertisement for the third time, alarm bells started ringing quite loudly. The closing date for the application was four o'clock that very afternoon. There was no time for pondering my situation any further as it was eleven o'clock already. Action was required and fast. I jumped from my seat, left my satchel with the library porter and ran to the government office. I completed the requisite application forms that afternoon with great trepidation.

As part of the entry requirements, I had to write an essay on 'English society' and take an oral test in English, chaired by two red-faced English gentlemen, whose accent was completely foreign to me. I placed no trust in a happy outcome. Hence, I told no one, not even my Beau-frère, my most trusted friend, that I had made an application for nurse training in my Mother Country. I continued with my private study in the library as usual and sat my GCE O Level examination during the first three weeks of June.

After the examination my life suddenly felt empty. I sought for the second time financial help from my younger brother-in-law so that I could pursue my GCE Advanced Level education. One Saturday I went again to his place in Rose Hill. I was lucky enough to meet my sister and Bissoon on their own. I explained to them my desperate financial situation, but once again I faced the brick wall.

Bissoon explained very politely his personal situation in the Company.

'If you wish I can have a word with my eldest brother, if you want a job as a salesman in one of our shops.'

I believed him. He was the fifth brother and he was an employee like the rest of the staff. But I did not want to work as a salesman in a garment shop. I thought a salesman's job was beneath my intelligence. Besides, I wanted to study full-time. It was a nightmare for me. I continued moving between Port Louis and my village home without any purpose. I was totally lost and did not know what my future held. In fact, I was in the deep pit of depression.

As a last resort I even started going to the Temple to pray to Hanumanji, even though I knew the Lord would not help me. I had to find a path by myself. I had no choice but to wait patiently for my O Level results. At first, I was very confident I would pass my examination. But after a few weeks, doubts started to seep through my skin and brain. To keep myself sane I helped Ma in the tobacco plantation and did odd jobs on our land. Although I was not happy staying at the village home, there was no other choice. I could not go on living in Port Louis being fed by my Brother-in-law. I was unemployed, and Mauritius did not have any facility to help individuals in my position with career advice or financial support. Apart from Ma, there was no one else who was willing to support and help me. I was in the same position as my brother when he was unemployed after failing his Cambridge School Certificate examination. I had thought that I would do better than him when the golden opportunity was given to me to commence my studies at the college. Now I thought I was a total failure and was going to end up just like my brother, humiliated and laughed at by the villagers.

One Sunday during the last week of June, I was with my sister and brother-in-law in Port Louis after having laboured all week in the field, when my sister handed me a small brown envelope.

'I received this envelope last week. I wanted to post it to you, but your Beau-frère kept forgetting it. He said the envelope is from one of the government's offices. It has a special stamp.'

'I am sorry,' said Beau-frère. 'I kept forgetting to post it. I hope it is not very important.'

My sister and my dear brother-in-law stood side by side looking at me, in great anticipation that I was going to tell them of its contents. It had the seal of the government. I had never received such a letter in my life. I opened the letter slowly and tentatively, feeling their piercing eyes.

To my great amazement I noted that the Matron of Blackburn Royal Infirmary, England, yes England, was pleased to offer me a place on the student nurse training course, due to commence on 3 October 1966. I had to confirm my acceptance by 1 July. The letter also informed me that the Foreign Office was paying eighty per cent of all my expenditure as I had performed quite well in the entrance examination. I looked at my sister and my brother-in-law in turn. I tried to say something to them, but the words would not come out of my dry mouth. I was stunned. Up to that point I had told nobody, not even my trusted brother-in-law. With great excitement I hugged my brother-in-law and my sister in turn and kissed the cheeks of my brother-in-law at least three times. Tears streamed down my cheeks.

'I am going to England.'

'What!' They exclaimed in unison with bewildered faces.

I handed the letter to my brother-in-law for his scrutiny. He scanned carefully through the lines.

'Well, what does it say?'

When, at last, I told them the full contents of the letter and its implications, they at first thought I was joking.

From that moment I knew my life had taken a new turning. As I was very apprehensive to tell Ma, I left it to my brother-in-law to release the news to her. Of course, Ma was devastated when I visited home on Monday with my brother-in-law. Beau-frère had taken a special day off to accompany me to Triolet. He was there to support Ma. We did not know how she would react to the news of me leaving her behind and travelling to a foreign country alone.

'How can you leave me?

I remained silent. She rushed at me poking her right fingers to my chest.

'How can you leave me, your Ma, who has given you everything?'

She accused me of not caring for her. She said she'd had a dream that I would succeed in my next examination. She was convinced I was better off in my own country than in a foreign one where I would have no family support. She accused me of ignoring the teaching of my Dadi that I should never leave Ma to travel to another country. She was too agitated to comprehend the reasons for my leaving. Beau-frère tried very hard to soothe her, but it was in vain.

'Don't worry, Jaysingh. She will accept the situation once she calms down.'

In the end, having carefully weighed the pros and cons of staying in Mauritius, I concluded I had no other choice but to ignore all her pleadings. As time went on, I became more convinced that my future lay elsewhere, where I would at least have a job and, above all, would be free from caste discrimination. The security of a regular income to support myself and my family was most appealing. And it would bring me some sort of dignity and self-respect, which I had been craving since my dismissal from the college.

In the end Ma reluctantly accepted my line of argument. I assured her I would definitely return home after three years, when I was fully qualified as a State Registered Nurse. I also promised her that, on my return, I would practise nursing in Mauritius and marry a Hindu Mauritian girl.

'You better start looking for a girl for me,' I joked. 'Three years will go very quickly, Ma.'

'What kind of girl should I look for?

'Oh, Ma, I want to marry an educated girl. She does not have to come from a rich family as long as she comes from a respectful family.'

'I know the very girl for you, Jaysingh. Do you want to see her before you leave?'

'Oh no Ma. Not yet. I am not ready to see any girls yet.'

Following this genuine response, Ma became more relaxed and started becoming fully involved in the preparations for my departure. During those three weeks I had many things to do which were new to me. While Ma was busy organising a puja to thank the Lords for my safe voyage and return, with the help of my brother-in-law, I planned the details of my voyage. I borrowed a black jacket from one of our neighbours for my passport photograph, because I didn't have one and Beau-Frère's was too loose as he was fairly tubby. I had to go to the Police Headquarters in Les Casernes, where the Passport Office was located, and complete a four-page form. I had to indicate who my nearest relative was. I knew

Ma was my nearest blood relative. However, I consciously decided not to insert her name, because if anything untoward happened to me, I did not want her to be informed first. Instead, without even asking the permission of my brother-in-law, I inserted his name on the form as nearest relative.

My British passport was ready for collection within five days. It was a very exciting moment when I held that dark blue passport in my hand with the shiny coat of arms indicating I was a British Subject Citizen of the United Kingdom and Colonies. The sight of the golden lion and silver unicorn standing proudly on the Royal Crown gave me added confidence that there was nothing for me to be afraid of in England as I was a proud British Citizen.

I booked my passage to England in a merchant ship, La Bourdonnais. I could not afford to fly by aeroplane, which would have taken me to England within twenty-four hours. I had no other choice but to travel by sea knowing full well that the journey would take three weeks. With the bursary money I bought two pairs of long trousers, three white long-sleeved shirts and a jacket. For the first time in my life, I bought myself black leather shoes. Ma and two of our neighbours ground roasted sweet corn on a special stone grinder for my sustenance, should I become hungry on my voyage.

Leaving my loved ones behind was not easy. I knew I was breaking one of the cherished wishes of my Dadi that I should never leave Ma behind. Her grief and tears streaming down her haggard cheeks were like arrows tearing my very conscience. During the week before my departure, our village house was buzzing with people. Many villagers came to see me and each one brought a present. I received a small shaving razor, a pen, writing pads and a leather wallet. And many neighbours gave me few rupees 'for a rainy day'. Various relatives I had not seen for a long while came over to bid good wishes to me. They were all very supportive of Ma, and kissed and hugged me before departing. Bissoon and Dev came over accompanied by Bissoon's mother and their two-week-old daughter, Kalyanee. On behalf of the Judoo Fils Company, he gave me an elegant blue blazer which had the Mauritian coat of arms, the Star and Key of the Indian Ocean. His mother donated me a dozen handkerchiefs with the monogram RW sewn at one of the corners. Beau-frère took me to Barclays bank and gave me £40 in traveller's cheques. It was mandatory that I had some cash with me to show that I was able to fend for myself for a while. While I was in Port Louis, I went to the famous Nalanda Bookshop and bought myself a one metre square map of the world. I thought the map would serve as a useful pointer along my journey.

On my last day I was both nervous and excited. One of my cousins took a photograph of me and Ma sitting on broken rattan chairs side by side on the veranda. We both looked morose, and the photograph showed weeks of tension gripping Ma's face. Bissoon took us to the seaport in his company van where I was surprised to see many villagers, my two sisters and some of our relatives waiting for us. Kissing and hugging each one of them was emotionally draining. I had to listen and nod to each and every Elder as if their advice was paramount to my future. When I made my final goodbyes and turned to leave, my sister Deomatee, who was clutching her two-weeks-old daughter, started singing one of my favourite Mukesh songs, '*O Janewale Ho Sake To Laut Ke Aana.*' (Oh traveller, please, come back home if you can.)

Everyone who was there to see me off joined in. It broke my heart to listen to them. I had been bottling up all my emotions, but that song wrenched at my whole being. With tears gushing down my cheeks, I rushed to Ma, hugged her again, then touched her feet.

'Forgive me Ma for leaving you behind. I will come back'.

With the Mukesh song ringing in my ears, I at last slowly climbed the gangplank of the ship, which was scheduled to very shortly take me away – I hoped to a land of plenty. My two brothers-in-law accompanied me on to the ship. At the end of the gangplank, I turned around to wave at my other relatives for one last time. It was hard seeing them crying and sobbing. The realisation that I was leaving my cherished loved ones behind was very painful to accept. I remembered Dadi relating to us how our grandfather had travelled in a merchant ship to visit his family in India and had never returned to Mauritius. He had died during the voyage and was cremated at sea without a proper Hindu ceremony. I sincerely hoped that I would not suffer such a dreadful fate and would be able to fulfil my ambition and my promises to Ma, my relatives and of course my dearest villagers.

I followed my two brothers-in-law, who were carrying my heavy brown leather cases, to my hammock in the lowest class of the ship. It was like climbing down an enormous pit. We had to manoeuvre four long staircases to reach our destination. There were other boys sitting on their hammocks, saying their farewells to relatives. I could not believe the suspended fabric was going to be my bed for the next three weeks. A few metres away from the hammocks there were thousands of bags of sugar and tea stacked in long rows as high as the eye could see. There were no cupboards to store my belongings. The only place to keep them was in my suitcase which was in turn pushed under the hammock. Both brothers-in-law hugged me and kissed me once again. Bissoon handed me a watch with a broad smile. That was a great surprise to me. I had never owned a watch until that moment. Beau-frère just stood there with tears streaming down his face.

'Jaysingh, take care my boy,' said Beau-frère. 'Be on your guard and choose your friends carefully. And please come back home when you finish your training. If at any time you need something, write to me. I shall always be here.'

His voice was trembling. He had done so much for me. I owed my future to him. I held him tight and kissed his cheeks again and again.

'Thank you for everything that you have done for me. I will try to follow the advice you have given me.'

When they left the ship, I sat on my hammock. I was on my own with strangers all around me and I realised the enormity of my decision. When the ship was ready to leave, I ran with the other boys to the top deck to bid my final farewell to Ma and my family. I frantically waved until their figures became small dots, and remained on deck until my beloved country disappeared in the ocean mist.

Chapter Twenty-Four

While these days passengers can fly nonstop in relative comfort and reach England within thirteen hours, my journey took over three weeks. For the whole journey my bed consisted of a hammock. I had fifteen companions, three Mauritians and the rest foreign nationals who later joined us at Mombasa. Instead of befriending Mauritians, I remained aloof and locked my thoughts within myself. I did not trust anyone.

In fact, throughout the journey I was scared for my safety, as all the boys were taller and better fed than me. At night it was difficult to sleep because of the suffocating heat and the scurrying of rats. I had to sleep with my shoes at the bottom end of the hammock in case the rats chewed them to pieces. To remain cool, we had to wear our shorts only. Several times a day we climbed four very steep staircases to the upper deck for our meals and to use the toilet facilities. For the first time it dawned on me that I was a very naive boy with very limited experience of life. While the other boys were jovial and could make friends easily, I felt isolated.

Since I could only eat fish and vegetables, my choice of diet was limited. The first time I was given a boiled egg for my breakfast, I did not know what it was until the cook explained to me. Dadi and Ma had instilled in me that the Hindu upper caste should always refrain from eating chicken, eggs, beef and pork. As for lamb I had never heard of it. This was not for the first time I had to make a hard choice. The cook had already warned me that unless I experiment with

European cuisine, like boiled potatoes, boiled cabbages, boiled and scrambled eggs, I would struggle to adjust in England.

'Why are you giving me these two white oval things on my plate?' I asked the cook quietly so that none of the boys would hear me.

He smiled.

'It is for you mon ami. It's your breakfast.'

'I do not eat such things.'

'But you must. I know you are a vegetarian. But you must try them. It is good for you.'

He raised both his arms and started flapping them and making clucking sounds, with broad smile on his face. At this point all the boys who were queuing behind me started laughing in chorus. I took it as friendly laughter.

'You try this and tell me if you like it.'

There were folding chairs and tables in the small, smelly canteen. The spoons, forks and condiments were stacked in a corner. I sat next to one of the small boys who had a friendly face. I had slowly started to gravitate towards him. He spoke fluent English. His father was a barrister in Mombasa and he had been accepted to study law in one of the London universities. I picked up the boiled egg, and was just about to place it in my mouth when the cook came running over and grabbed my hand, muttering and shaking his head.

'No, No. Mon Ami. You have to décortiquer l'oeuf first.'

I looked at him, baffled. 'Décortiquer l'oeuf premier, mon ami?'

He sat down opposite me and demonstrated the technique of shelling. This was an illuminating experience. I quietly muttered a plea for Ma's forgiveness, as I thought what I was going to do was wrong. But since I was only transgressing in a small way, I was sure she would understand. When the cook picked a knife and cut the egg into three equal slices, I could not refuse. I doubt whether he realised how rotten I felt for having shed twenty years of culinary principle.

'Have you never had eggs?' A Creole Mauritian asked me.

'No. We kept chickens, but we always sold the eggs to our neighbours or the merchants. I was forbidden to eat such things.'

'It is good for you. My father who is a teacher told me eggs are the favourite food of English people. Are you a vegetarian?'

'No. I eat fish.'

With the encouragement of my Creole friend, I subsequently progressed to eating chicken and lamb without undergoing similar heartache or attacks of conscience. However, I refused to experiment with beef and pork. I could not eat them. Eating beef, in particular, was against the Hindu religion. I could not abandon all my long-held principles. Rejection of beef and pork helped me to maintain some of the values and beliefs of my Hindu identity.

From six in the morning until eight in the evening the passengers of fourth class were allowed to freely roam about on the upper deck at the stern of the ship. As it was hot and humid inside the compartment, it was a relief to wander about on deck. I spent many hours every day admiring the might and beauty of the sea, its deep blue colour and the trail of white froth being formed along the sides of the ship and was mesmerised by the sheer agility of the dolphin pod that tried to swim alongside.

These beautiful sights helped to lift my spirits, which were being shredded by homesickness. The rest of the deck was fenced off to us. We could see the other passengers but were unable to communicate with them. In the evening we had a free view of the lives of the upper-class passengers. We watched them in their suits and glittering dresses, sitting in groups and eating their sumptuous meals, while their lips moved nonstop and their heads nodded in each other's direction. They seemed always to be holding a glass of wine, as if their personal identity depended on how much they could consume of that red liquid.

Saturday evenings were the best occasions of all. On the first-class deck, men and women danced by holding each other closely and at times I could see them kissing passionately. I must admit it did stir my manhood instincts. Although I was twenty years old, besides my sister, I had never held a girl in my arms. It was a taboo for boys to even touch a village girl. Watching these men and women together I would often have the sweet thought of holding a girl in my arms. I wondered what it would be like to hold her hand and touch her face. But I knew I had a long wait, for according to my upbringing such close encounters with the opposite sex could only be carried out after marriage. I resolved I would never hold a girl unless she was chosen by my family. Moreover, I was constantly reminded of the Hindu principles and the teachings of Dadi and Ma. I was, of course, envious of those passengers who seemed to be leading a luxurious life on the first-class deck of the ship. I wanted to lead a life like them and live like them.

After ten days of sailing, we arrived at Mombasa. Following so many days of being cooked in the bottom of the ship, we were all excited to get out and feel the land under our feet again. We were given a three-hour pass to visit the centre of Mombasa, if we so wished. As nearly all the passengers were taking up the offer, I joined the other Mauritians reluctantly for the six-mile walk to the centre of town. The passengers from the other decks, I noticed, were being ferried by taxis.

To my surprise I found Mombasa to be very pleasant. We were spellbound by the size of the four enormous gleaming white elephant tusks that criss-crossed the dual carriageway, dramatically marking the entrance to the city. The streets were wide, and a variety of flowers lined the edges of the pavements. There were Asians everywhere. I could not believe my eyes when I saw them selling curries and boiled rice by the road. My friends each bought a plate of curry and rice topped with chilli sauce and also bought a plate for me. I was very grateful to them, as I did not have any Kenyan currency with me. We sat under some palm trees by the road and ate that food with the greatest pleasure. While we were enjoying ourselves, a group of young African girls approached us. One of them, who had a beautiful smile on her face, sat next to me.

'Hi, do you want to see some extraordinary views of Mombasa?'

While she was talking to me, I could see she was shifting her short skirt higher and higher. Suddenly she got hold of my left hand and placed it on her right breast.

'I can show you the rest if you come with me.'

I was horrified at such a suggestion. Although the other boys decided to join the girls, I declined.

'Come on, Jaysingh. This is the time to show the world that we have grown up. Forget your parents. Let us enjoy ourselves.'

I glared at them and left to their own devices. Instead of visiting the shops and other tourist places, I returned to the ship on my own. I was teased by the boys later for missing a golden opportunity to savour the delights of African beauties, but I remained determined never to be mixed up with prostitutes.

We stayed at the Mombasa seaport for the day then travelled to Djibouti. We were not allowed to disembark when we reached Djibouti for reasons not made known to us, although passengers from the upper decks were seen stretching themselves onshore. Our journey then took us through the Suez Canal, which I had been waiting to see with great anticipation. I vividly recall the ship slowly moving along the canal. We were all on the deck waiving at the Egyptian children who shouted at us in a language I could not understand. I watched in fascination as they grabbed at items thrown from the first-class deck of the ship. It helped remind me that poverty was common throughout the world and I was no exception in my suffering.

We disembarked at Marseille on 16 September having left Mauritius on 22 July 1966. With my pre-booked ticket, I travelled through the night on the French TGV train to Calais and from there in a hovercraft to Folkestone. It was both nerve-racking and exciting to manoeuvre from one mode of transport to another with my heavy suitcases. I had seen people travelling by train in Hindi films, and here I was sampling for the first time in my life this vast steel engine speeding along at over a hundred miles an hour carrying thousands of passengers. I could have stayed overnight in Paris but that would have meant cashing one of my traveller's cheques to pay for food and accommodation. I was not prepared to squander the hard-earned money by sightseeing in Paris and was anxious to reach my destination as soon as possible.

I arrived at Folkestone harbour on 17 September 1966. Dark clouds were hanging low in the sky, and I was shivering from the cold. I left the ship carrying my heavy suitcases. I was only eight stone in body weight, with a waist of twenty-eight inches – as thin as a bean stalk. Looking back, I have difficulty in imagining how I managed to transport those suitcases and find my way around. Yet there I was in my mother country safe and sound after nearly three weeks of arduous journeying, but too tired to admire the surroundings.

I reached London but had no idea where Blackburn was. Everything around me looked big and overwhelming. I was totally confused. I was horrified to find that white people were cleaning the train and the pavements. I had always imagined that such privileged people lived in great mansions, and only their servants carried out such menial jobs.

Euston station was packed with thousands of commuters rushing around. Nobody seemed to have time for anybody else. I was hungry and desperate to find my connection to Blackburn. I had no idea how long I just stood on the platform between my suitcases in a disorientated state.

'Are you Runjitsingh Woogara?'

Somebody was tapping my shoulder. I turned and saw a smartly dressed man staring at me. He was holding a clipboard in his hand.

'Yes, I am.'

'Ah. Good. I am from the Mauritian High Commission and am here to help you. I understand this is your first visit to the UK. Let us go to the waiting room, and I will give you further information about your itinerary.'

I was mightily relieved to meet him and shake his cold hand. I had no idea that anybody was scheduled to meet me. He bought me a cup of coffee and sandwiches as he must have realised, I was starving. He explained his role and said he wanted me to stay overnight to rest my body. He emphasised that there was no need to hurry and travel to my destination that night. However, in the end, as he realised my determination to reach my destination at the earliest opportunity, he helped me buy a one-way train ticket to Blackburn and stayed with me until I boarded the correct train. I was so touched by the help and support of the employee of the Mauritius High Commission that I wrote a lengthy letter to the High Commissioner expressing my deepest gratitude.

Chapter Twenty-Five

I reached Blackburn Royal Infirmary at around two in the morning. The taxi driver dropped me at the nurses' residence. I had changed all my traveller's cheques in London to pay for my London to Blackburn journey, and after the taxi fare I was left with only £10 in my pocket. The enormous black metal gates of the nurses' residence looked like the castle gates I had seen in a black and white film at home in my village. They were shut and there was nobody around. The gates were at least fifty metres away from the main building. Although I knew it was useless to shake them and make a loud noise, I carried on in this frantic pursuit.

It was obvious that nobody expected my arrival. Here I was on my own in the middle of the night, having arrived at my final destination after three weeks of laborious journeying. I must have been waiting by the gate for nearly two hours before a woman walked up to the gate. I was relieved to see both her and the metal key in her hand. In broken English I explained I was there to start my nurse training.

'But this is a female residence,' she replied, having at last deciphered my meaning. 'The male nurses' home is at Queen's Park, which is one mile from here.'

I was totally confused. I had presumed that the male residence would be at the Royal Infirmary. Besides, how was I going to make my way to Queen's Park Hospital? The taxi had long gone.

‘I was told to report to the Blackburn Royal Infirmary. I am very tired. Please would you inform somebody of my arrival?’ I pleaded.

By that time rain had started falling quite hard. The rain on my back felt very different to the rain I was used to. In Mauritius the tropical rain is normally quite warm and often soothing to the body. I had no raincoat to protect me. I had started feeling very cold and my body was twitching. I had not eaten all evening as the price of food in the train was prohibitive. In the end the nurse managed to call somebody. I had to wait another half hour before the Assistant Matron appeared on the scene. She was a tall lady in her fifties, wearing a brilliant white, starched, tightly-fitting uniform with a frilly cap. She looked very stern to me with her austere, upright posture. It so happened she was expecting me, but as she reminded me many times I was not supposed to arrive until 3 October when the training was due to start. She noted my dishevelled appearance and realised my state of desperation. She asked me to escort her, but as my suitcases were rather heavy, I had a problem keeping up with her as we climbed two staircases to reach a tiny bedroom on the third floor.

Once I was in the room, she looked at me sternly.

‘You are in the female residence, Mr Woogara. Males are not allowed in this area. I have made an exception for you because you looked so tired. You should not wander about. You can sleep here and I’ll call for you at nine in the morning.’

On her way out she showed me the toilet facilities then vanished. It must have been five in the morning by then. I felt vulnerable and cursed myself for not staying overnight in London. My naivety was glaringly obvious. I missed my family bitterly. I wanted to lean on somebody and cry my heart out, but there was nobody around. I was on my own, desolate, exhausted to my very bones and ravenous. I realised how silly I was for not eating anything on the train. I opened and shut all the drawers, but there was nothing to eat. I drank a glassful of water and was at the point of lying on the soft mattress when I realised there was something for me to eat. I swiftly opened my suitcase and there was the plastic bag, tucked under all my clothes, my saviour, the sweet corn.

'Just mix the sweet corn flour with some cold water and you will have a ready meal,' Ma had said. There was water in the room but Ma had forgotten to give me a dish and I could not find any container. In desperation I scooped up the dry meal with my fingers and dropped it into my mouth. For ease of swallowing, I drank plenty of water. I must have had at least ten scoops before my hunger was satisfied. At that moment I was eternally grateful to Ma for providing me with the ready meal. I had been very reluctant to bring the bundle with me and had laughed at the very idea of carrying such a substance.

'England is a very rich country, Ma. They have plenty of food. I'll be earning enough money to buy anything I need. It is a waste of time carrying such a thing with me.'

'You never know what tomorrow brings, my son. It is only to meet your needs in an emergency.'

It was nearly morning when I finished eating. I knew the Assistant Matron would be calling for me in three hours, but I had not slept lying down for nearly two days. I threw myself on top of the mattress in my full gear. I was disturbed by loud knocks and banging on the door. It was strange feeling when I tried to get out of the bed. For the last three weeks the hammock would swing around until I steadied myself with my feet on the deck of the ship. I had totally lost my bearings and could not figure out who was making that horrible loud noise.

'Mr Woogara, are you awake?'

It finally dawned on me about my environment and that I had achieved my aim of arriving safely in England. Realising my position, I quickly opened the door and there was the Assistant Matron, looking as if she had been there all the time keeping guard on her female nurses in case of an attack by Woogara.

'Sorry, Matron, to keep you waiting. Please, can you give me few more minutes?'

I was escorted with all my belongings to the dining room where I was presented with a full English breakfast. I had never seen the pink, fleshy strips and round, brown elongated objects before. Every morning on the ship, my breakfast consisted of one boiled egg and two pieces of toast followed by a mug of tea. On Sundays we were presented with a bowl of cereal and milk. I asked the waiter what they were.

'Bacon and sausages, mate,' he replied rolling his eyes.

I had no idea what he meant by bacon and sausages or to be precise what kind of meat they were. I did not ask any more questions because I did not want to show any further ignorance. I just emptied the plate. They tasted good and I ate them with great relish. Later that morning the Assistant Matron came to see me accompanied by a Mauritian boy called Jimmy.

'Jimmy is going to show you the ropes. Matron will drive you to the YMCA where you will stay until you find your own accommodation. Tomorrow you are going to start working as a nursing auxiliary in the ENT ward until 3 October when you start your nurse training proper.'

I had no idea what she meant by nursing auxiliary or ENT.

About ten in the morning Matron drove me to the YMCA accompanied by Jimmy. She was a middle-aged lady with gentle manners and showed a good understanding of my situation. She conversed with me slowly and placed great stress on her accent. She assured me that I would be well looked after during my training. Obviously, I expressed my gratitude although I had no idea what she meant by the words 'I shall be well looked after.' She dropped us at the YMCA and left me in the company of Jimmy.

Jimmy was a tall, muscular man with shiny black hair that was combed neatly backwards. He was dressed in a black suit and was wearing a big, flashy, red tie in a loose knot. He had a thin moustache and a gentle smile on his face. He acted and behaved like the famous Indian actor, Raj Kapoor. He had very fair skin and in fact looked like the actor in many respects. I could tell he was very proud of his looks. Instead of talking to me in Creole he started conversing in BBC English. Undoubtedly, he was well versed with the British culture and pattern of life. Once I was settled in my YMCA room, he asked if I had enjoyed my meal in the hospital.

'Yes, I did. I was very hungry. By the way Jimmy, what is bacon and sausages?'

'Well, they're bits of pigs. I love them. Did you?'

I felt the blood drain from my face and started convulsing. I had eaten pigs. It was against my Hindu upbringing to eat pigs or cows. I was a vegetarian, and with the exception of fish, that was my diet before I left my Island. I knew I had started shedding my Hindu principles, as I had sampled lamb, chicken and eggs while travelling in the merchant ship. But I thought I had now gone too far.'

'I had no idea it was pig's meat, Jimmy. Had I known I would not have eaten it. I was a vegetarian before I left home.'

'You can't stay a vegetarian in this country, Runjitsingh. You must eat everything or else you won't survive. Look at me. I don't think I am a Mauritian anymore; I am a British citizen, and girls love it because I have become part of the British culture.'

'By the way Jimmy, please call me by my home name, 'Jaysingh.' I do not like to be called by the name I have been registered with at birth. It's so impersonal.'

'You have to change your name. Look at me. At home they used to call me Janesh. Don't you think Jimmy sounds better than Janesh?'

'Why did you change your name?'

'The British like everything that is familiar to them. It will be awkward for them to pronounce 'Jaysingh. Now 'Andrew' is a good name. It sounds sexy too.'

'I don't want an English name. I am a Hindu. I do not want to lose my identity.'

'Well, I am going to call you 'Jay' from now on.'

I had been only one full day in England and I had gained a new identity.

This was my first lesson. In order to survive in England, according to Jimmy, I had to abandon the sacred Hindu principles I had assimilated during my childhood and take a moniker that would be acceptable to the British tongue.

Despite his advice, I swore to myself I would never eat pork or beef. I would try to maintain my Hindu culture as long as I could. I thought total assimilation of European culture was wrong. I was not there to please the British girls. Despite my freedom, I was determined to respect my family tradition.

I felt lonely at the YMCA after Jimmy left me. It was too much for my system to decipher my new cultural surroundings. Everything looked big and different. Doubts kept creeping in about whether I would be able to survive.

'How are you going to cope, Jaysingh, in this new world?' I asked myself, looking at my reflection in the mirror of the bedroom.

I had not realised I would miss my family so much. I was in the deep abyss of homesickness. I felt bewildered and confused. I dearly missed my brother-in-law, with whom I could share any inner feelings that were tormenting me. I had been tossed about from one house to another: Triolet, Saint Paul, Port Louis, the public library. During the last five years I had lost any sense of permanency. I no longer knew where my sweet home was. I really thought the isolation I had experienced in Mauritius would have prepared me to face my new world. But reality often fails to match one's expectations, and that first night I felt so alone I tucked my penknife under my pillow in case I was attacked.

Chapter Twenty-Six

Next day I reported to the hospital as advised. Following a lengthy preliminary interview with the Assistant Matron, and before I signed an employment contract to work as an auxiliary nurse until 3 October, I had a medical. The male doctor gave me a thorough examination. During the examination he asked me to remove my trousers and bend forward until my head touched my knees.

'Well, tell me. Do you like girls or boys?'

'What do you mean Doctor? All my friends at home have been boys. I was never allowed to fraternise with girls.'

'I mean have you ever slept with boys?'

I at last realised what he was getting at. 'No, doctor, I'm not a homosexual.'

'Well then, you have passed the medical.'

Donned in a white uniform, I was sent to start my duties in the Ear, Nose and Throat (ENT) ward. I was given no training and was not informed what the work entailed. For the first time in my life, without any prior preparation, I had to clean patients' bottoms, bathe them under supervision, clean their mouths with swabs and learn to make beds without any creases. Undertaking such tasks was, at first, traumatic. I was brought up in an environment where only women could do such things. They were not part of a man's work. Although I felt humiliated and ashamed, I kept these feelings to myself. I was determined to finish my nurse training, even if it meant doing things that were repulsive to me. I had already sacrificed too much by leaving my family. I could not shatter their expectations of me. The nurses were very helpful. Once I related my background to them, they were always willing to show me what to do and support me. I was surrounded by female nurses. Even though I was assigned to a male ward, there was not a single male nurse. In Mauritius I had been told that only male nurses worked in male wards and females on female wards.

Over the next few weeks, I learned the routine of the ward. Gradually, I was becoming more confident. I felt it was good preparation for my real nurse training. I started taking pride in my work and was bent on showing the staff that despite my naivety I could become an important member of the ward team.

Unfortunately, leaping the cultural boundary in one bound was not easy. One Friday morning, when the ward was very busy, the telephone rang in the ward sister's office. It continued to ring for a little while. I knew I was the only available person to answer it, but I was scared to touch it. I had never spoken on the phone with anybody in my life. In our village and even at my sister's house in Port Louis there was no telephone, and therefore there was no need for me to have any knowledge of them. In the end I walked into Sister's office, picked up the phone and said 'Hello', as I had seen others do. I knew somebody was trying to say something on the other end of the line, but for the life of me I could not figure out what they were saying. I quickly dropped the phone and pretended nothing had happened. Half an hour later I was told I must go and see Matron that very instant.

Matron was sitting in her lavish office. She smiled at me when I walked in and was very courteous. Before I sat down, she informed me it was her on the other end of the telephone line that morning.

'Why did you not answer it?' she asked, perplexed. 'I wanted to leave an important message for Sister.'

'I'm sorry, Matron. I could not understand what was being said. I panicked.' Then I related to her my dilemma of never having been exposed to telephones.

Once Matron learned my handicap, she showed great understanding towards me and was arranged various informal teaching sessions to improve my skill in handling telephone calls.

After three weeks work as an auxiliary nurse, I received a cheque. It was a great moment in my life; I was thrilled and thanked God for my good fortune. I knew then that I had made the right decision to come to England. 'I have a job,' I shouted. 'I can now help my family.'

I practically ran to the bank to cash it. Twenty pounds in crisp new notes was a lot of money, but instead of buying some winter clothes for myself as I was advised by the Matron, I bought a £10 postal order and sent it to my beloved Beau-frère. I was determined to pay back his debt of £40 as quickly as possible.

During my first week at work, I had stayed at the YMCA. I paid a week in advance for my board and lodging, which included breakfast and an evening meal. I thought it was rather expensive and the place was at least two miles away from the hospital. Although the hospital was situated along a bus route, I preferred to walk. It saved on the bus fares and the walk from town to the hospital gave me an ideal opportunity to observe British society. One morning, I was walking to work wearing the black gabardine overcoat provided by the hospital, when I heard yelling from a group of young men who were walking.

'Eh, black Paki. Go back to your fu***** country. You smell. We don't want you in our country.'

I turned around noticed there were five of them. They were white and walking fast towards me. The street was deserted as it was quite early in the morning. At the sound of their vicious tone, adrenaline poured through my body. I knew they were going to attack me. I had always been a good runner and within seconds my feet left the spot with such energy there was no way they would have caught me. I ran all the way to the hospital without stopping. It was my first welcoming lesson from British society. I had read in books that British men behaved like gentlemen. But this was reality. I genuinely thought I had left the evils of racial discrimination behind in Mauritius. How wrong I was!

I related the incident to Jimmy. I was genuinely scared of walking along that street again. He was very supportive and advised me to take a different route. From that day onwards, with the help of Jimmy, I started looking for a place to rent nearer the hospital. Jimmy lived close to the hospital and had a good idea of the surrounding area. That evening we knocked on several doors, but nobody was willing to entertain us. Most shut their doors once they found out our intention.

'We don't rent to Pakis.' One lady told us.

By Sunday afternoon I was desperate to find a place. I was walking along a road and saw an elderly lady weeding her front garden. I stopped.

'You have nice flowers. What are those red roses called?'

Before she replied I told her I was a nurse and was working at the infirmary. She gave me a warm smile and asked me to come closer. I opened the gate, went to the flower bed, bent on my knees and took long a whiff. That gesture transported my body and soul to when my dear Dadi tried to smell the rose at that big house near our village.

'Oh, it has a beautiful smell,' I said, and related to her the story of my dear Dadi. As I was walking out, I mentioned to her that I was looking for a place to rent so I could be nearer to the hospital.

'I live on my own, and this is a three-bedroom house. I suppose you could live in one of the rooms.'

'Oh, thank you.'

Serendipity had opened its wide arms again, and I was happy as a lark. With a monthly rent of £7, I had my own room and all the facilities of the kitchen to cook my meals. I had a caring landlady and felt safe in that room. I was ready to conquer the world.

Chapter Twenty-Seven

I commenced my nurse training on 3 October 1966. It was held at Queen's Park Hospital, as Blackburn Royal Infirmary did not have its own training school. I could not wait to start the course. I had been thinking of this day non-stop since my arrival in the UK. I reported quite early to the training school, excited and apprehensive. There were thirty-nine of us in the cohort and only two of us were male. Nearly all of the trainees were under the age of twenty and had graduated to full nurse training from being a cadet nurse.

Cadet nursing was quite popular at that time. Those students who had slipped the rungs of the GCE O Level examination and failed to gain even three passes were able to start nursing as a cadet from the age of sixteen. The new recruits were greeted enthusiastically by Miss Frankland who was going to be our tutor for the next eighteen months. She was a tiny, slim lady of about forty years with a baby-like face. But by Jove she could project her voice, and she was a strict disciplinarian.

My three weeks employment as an Auxiliary Nurse had helped me to shed some of the shields around my shyness, which had hampered me since my childhood. I was now able to converse with my female colleagues without feeling any discomfort. Although the cohort had mini groups of its own, I was never left on my own and everyone took great pains to encourage me to join them. The other male was from Ghana, but the girls, for some reason, showed greater affinity for me.

I remained wary of them, however, and maintained a degree of aloofness.

I applied myself to studying the principles and practice of nursing with great determination. For the first time in my life, I could afford to purchase my own books as I was paid around £27 a month. We were also provided with free drinks and one main meal during the day. Since I hardly went anywhere in the evening, I was able to save the bulk of my monthly income. My female colleagues tried several times to persuade me to join them at the night clubs. But I always made some sort of excuse. Even Jimmy gave up on me.

I spent hours in the hospital library, researching the medical and nursing subjects we were studying at that time. Although I had never studied Biology or General Science, I coped with all aspects of the nursing studies fairly well and passed my preliminary examinations without much difficulty. All except cookery. For cookery lessons we had to attend the local college. We were taught how to boil carrots, potatoes, cabbage and to steam fish.

We undertook various role-plays. One of them being to feed each other, with one partner pretending to be a very ill patient. We also had to learn how to set the table for the patient's dinner. The examination consisted of two parts: theory of nutrition and a practical examination. To my great surprise, I came out first in the theoretical aspect of cookery, with a mark of ninety. Sadly, I scored only twenty marks on the practice of cooking and was the bottom candidate.

In the practical examination we were asked to poach an egg, boil a carrot and make rice pudding within a limited time. I had no idea what I had to do to poach an egg. It was the first time I had heard that term. I was able to boil the carrot but did not know how to poach the egg and make the rice pudding. During the examination one of the girls kept signalling me. She even passed a note to me depicting the techniques. But I was still there after two hours trying to poach my egg and prepare the rice pudding. In the end the teacher had to stop me. By this time all my colleagues had left the college.

I was very embarrassed when the teacher sat beside me. I explained to her that my ignorance came from my cultural upbringing and the type of food we ate. She showed great understanding and was very empathetic. Before I left, she showed me how to poach an egg and make a delicious rice pudding. While none of my colleagues had the opportunity to taste their own cooking, I was invited to sample the egg and the rice pudding. They were delicious. When the cookery result was published, I was even more surprised to learn I had passed the practical cookery part of the examination.

Within four months I had repaid all the money I had borrowed from my brother-in-law. As I promised myself, I started routinely sending money to Ma. During pay week, with great elation, I made my monthly trip to the post office and sent £8 by postal order to Ma. This was a great moment in my life. I knew the money would be her saviour as she was still paying the debt for the weddings of my sister and brother. Although she had never asked me directly for any money, I felt it was my obligation to help her. I was still feeling guilty for having left her behind and this was my way of redeeming myself.

After twelve weeks of learning the theory of nursing, we were all sent to the clinical wards for six months to practise, under the supervision of the trained ward staff, what we had been taught in the classroom. We had regular visits from a clinical teacher who taught us difficult procedures. She was there to help and support us should we face any untoward problems on the ward. My first clinical placement was on a male orthopaedic ward. I was proud to be part of the ward team dressed in my neatly ironed white uniform. Any tasks that were allocated to me I ensured were completed with care and dedication. I was there to learn and did not hesitate to ask questions of my supervisor. I was happy in the ward environment, as I knew help was at hand should I face any difficulties.

However, there were some things that happened on the wards that still torment me at times. Subtle racial discrimination from some of the trained staff was quite common. I was often allocated to clean bed pans and feed patients when other student nurses from my group were shown complicated procedures such as the setting up an intravenous infusion or catheterisation. A more overt form of discrimination was the refusal by some patients to be nursed by me. One evening I approached a male patient with the 'back trolley' which was used to carry soap, water and towels to relieve the pressure points on the back and improve blood supply.

'Blackie, don't come near me. You go to your own country. I do not want to be touched by you.'

The patient persisted in this mode, encouraging other patients to join him. He was adamant I was alien to him, and would not let me help him. My embarrassment was saved by the sudden appearance of the ward sister, who gave the patient just ten minutes to choose between being looked after by me or leaving the ward. In the end the patient calmed down and, with Sister standing by his side with a stern face, even apologised for his behaviour.

Ordeals like this occurred several times during my training, and after I finished, but in due course I learnt to live with the embarrassment. At first it hurt me: those abusive words felt like arrows piercing my body. I spent many sleepless nights trying to think of methods to cope with them. In Mauritius I had been a victim of caste discrimination, and I genuinely thought I had escaped it by coming to the mother country. But to my great astonishment and frustration, in many ways it was worse here. I not only experienced overt and covert racial discrimination on the wards, it was also rampant on the streets of Blackburn. I was frightened to venture to town on my own, and felt much safer when accompanied Jimmy and his friend Raj. They were bolder than me and were not prepared to accept abuse from anybody. However, it made me determined to show anyone who was abusive towards me that I was not a threat to them. I wanted to win this battle of overt racial discrimination by being pleasant and friendly towards my tormentors instead of showing any signs of aggression. As Mahatma Gandhi taught, the threat of violence can be conquered through peaceful means.

Chapter Twenty-Eight

My determination to succeed during my nurse training somehow isolated me from my own colleagues and British society at large. After being in the UK for nearly two years I still had no idea what happened outside the hospital environment. During this time, I maintained a simple routine: work and study in the hospital library.

My introvert personality was a source of great handicap to me. At this time of my life my interaction with the opposite sex was minimal. I got on well with my female colleagues. They were all very willing to help me if I asked any questions. But I had never asked any of them out to the pub or to a nightclub.

However, there was one particular nurse, junior to me, who appeared very interested in my wellbeing and the country of my birth. Her name was Sandra, and she was tall, with long, blonde hair. We had several passing conversations in the dining room, and once or twice she tried to engage me in a friendly chat. But I never paid her close attention and often deliberately avoided her. I was reluctant to be involved with any girls because, in fact, I was scared of them.

One day I was changing in the locker room for an afternoon shift and heard a rustling sound behind me. There she was, standing erect in her starched uniform, smiling at me. I was rather surprised as the female changing room was located on the opposite side of the corridor.

'Hi Sandra, you look well. In which ward you are working today.' I asked her, my voice trailing away.

‘We are in the same ward. It’s exciting! Is it not?’

‘So, you are allocated to Nightingale Ward as well? How interesting.’

Every twelve weeks we had to change wards to gain varied experience. My last ward was a surgical ward. I had greatly benefited from the experience of caring for surgical patients and was quite emotional on my last day. That day I was rather anxious, because it was going to be my first day on a medical ward. I had heard many tales about the senior sister from a colleague, who portrayed her as very dragon-like. Although I had often tried to avoid Sandra, I was a bit relieved to discover a familiar face would be on the same ward.

During my twelve weeks on Nightingale Ward, Sandra was very supportive. She was more practical than I was, and was always ready to help me with the aseptic technique, back round, and the dreaded medicine round, when we, the junior student nurses, had to accompany the sister. During such rounds the sister frequently asked me the effects and side effects of the current prescribed drugs. Sandra was often quick to my rescue and forwarded the answers before I had time to formulate a reply.

‘I did not ask you, Nurse Nicholson.’

‘Sorry, Sister. I thought you asked me,’ Sandra would reply, eyeing me surreptitiously.

Somehow, Sandra always managed to obtain the same break period as mine. And I frequently found myself in her company when I least expected it. One day, when we were eating our lunch in the dining room following a very busy morning, she politely asked me whether I would like to come to her house as it was her sister's birthday.

I looked at her with great surprise, dumbfounded. Up to then, I had never been anywhere except the hospital and the room I rented, which was only three hundred yards away.

I raised my eyes and looked at her eagerly for the first time. She was smiling and giggling, her even, white teeth showing between her lips as they moved in laughter. She kept shuffling her glasses on her nose.

'Well, Sandra.' I sighed, taking a long, deep breath. 'I'll definitely think about it and will let you know.'

'But her birthday is tomorrow, Jay. Today is Friday. I won't be able to see you again before then.'

Although I was called 'Jaysingh' at home in Mauritius I decided that everybody in the UK should address me as 'Jay'. Jimmy thought the suffix 'Singh' gave away too easily that I was a foreigner. 'Jay' was a neutral name, and he persuaded me to call myself by my new nickname.

'Sandra,' I said in desperation. 'I have never been to anybody's house and I won't know what is expected of me. I may spoil your sister's party. Besides, I won't know how to get to your place, because I have never been outside Blackburn on my own.'

While I was uttering these words, my stomach was quivering. I was imagining myself, a coloured man, walking alone on the streets of Accrington while glaring eyes peered at me from white sockets. I was very uneasy at the thought of leaving my safe and secure environment.

'Oh, don't worry Jay. I'll wait for you at Blackburn bus station at three o'clock and we shall go together. My sister is really looking forward to meeting you. Please say you will come.'

She left me no other choice. She had thought of everything. Since I did not want to upset her, I said 'okay'. She grabbed me and hugged me in full view of the other diners. I was so embarrassed, I immediately left the dining room and rushed to the loo to reflect on the consequences of that key word, 'okay'.

Next day, I was approaching the bus station at the appointed time and saw her, in the distance, waiting for me in a blue skirt and a white blouse. The sight of her sent shivers through my veins to such an extent that I lost my nerve all together and ran home without meeting her.

When I saw her on the ward the following day, she asked me several times why was I not interested in her and whether I had a girlfriend in Mauritius. I apologised for letting her down and made various excuses, none of them very convincing. After that she lost interest in me, and I could go back to focusing on my work. I know now it was an unforgivable act to leave her waiting for me at the station. But I did not want to be involved with English girls and start a serious relationship that could lead to breaking my solemn promises to Ma.

Chapter Twenty-Nine

The second year of training was a very busy time for all of us. I was immersed in my studies and in my practical work on different wards. Wearing the second-year bands on my epaulette was an experience in itself, as the junior students started to respect my seniority. It also meant I was the first to go for my lunch break and could now sit on the same rows as staff nurses. Of course, I was very envious of my senior colleagues and knew the only way to be like them was to continue concentrating on my studies and pass my six-monthly examination.

In August I received a very sad letter from my brother, Hemsingh, in Mauritius, which completely unbalanced me. He had been unemployed for six months and was having great difficulty in finding a suitable job. The villagers were jeering at him, as he was again working as a labourer in the sugarcane fields. He begged me to remove him from such a humiliating situation by finding him a student nurse training post in England.

The letter left me in utter turmoil. My brother was a married man and had a one-year-old-daughter. Above all, my dear mother was living with them, although she was still able to support herself by working as a labourer and keeping a cow and several goats. My increased allowance had not deterred her from the chores she had been doing nearly all her married life. My sister-in-law was keeping house and was fully dependent on my mum and my brother as she was unqualified to do anything else. I did not know what to do. My second-year examination was looming and I could not concentrate on my study. There was a clear policy at the hospital that close relatives, such as siblings, were not allowed to be employed. All of us at the hospital had accepted that policy and had never questioned it.

After three days of sheer hell, worried and frustrated, a stratagem emerged. I decided to see Matron and make her realise I was a very unhappy person as I had no friends I could relate to and was continuously homesick and missing my family. I went to her and pleaded with her to offer a student nurse training position to a male cousin of mine so that I would be happier. My sad demeanour and tearful expression won her heart, and then and there she offered my brother State Enrolled Nurse training, a more limited course than mine as he possessed only two subjects at the Cambridge School Certificate. I was relieved and very happy, but also sad that my brother was leaving behind his wife, daughter and Ma. But I concluded it was a sacrifice worth taking. As a qualified professional he could return to Mauritius after three years and obtain a job in one of the hospitals. Besides, he would be earning sufficient money to support his family. Moreover, he would no longer be the subject of humiliating jeers by his own peers. I had been in that position and did not want my brother to suffer in the same way. I immediately sent him a sum of money from my savings that could buy him suitable winter clothes and a ticket for the sea voyage.

Prior to my brother's arrival, I started looking for accommodation that could house both of us. Luck was still shining on me; a junior male nurse from Mauritius had given notice that he was terminating his nurse training. He had decided nursing was not for him and was returning to the island. His flat was near to the hospital. It had a bunk bed, an electric radiator, direct access from the busy trunk road and the landlady and landlord were very agreeable people. I did not do any cooking at my present flat, as I mainly relied on fish and chips and one main meal in the hospital canteen. I was too timid to cook and worried that the smell of curry would upset my landlady. So, I was not concerned that the kitchen in this new flat was situated beyond the lounge. I was doubly pleased to find out the monthly rent was less than I was paying at my present place.

My brother arrived in England during the first week of January 1968, ready to commence his nurse training the following week. I went to meet him at Blackburn Railway Station. It was great to see him, but he looked very thin and haggard and was wearing a cream summer suit. I explained to him about my lies to the matron, and that he could only save my embarrassment if he told nobody he was my brother. From that day I started addressing him as my cousin "Harry".

When we arrived at the flat, he was not very pleased.

'Are we going to live in this tiny room? You don't even have proper beds.'

I was surprised that he had forgotten our childhood days so easily when we six of us were living in a two-bed roomed leaky thatched house. It was a shock to him that after nearly two years in the UK I could only afford to live as a pauper.

When I explained to him that Mother Country was not a land of honey he calmed down.

'I'll take the bottom bunk,' said my brother. 'You can sleep on the top.'

We talked nearly all night, only stopping when we were both too worn out to listen to each other anymore. I was happy to have him as a companion.

My brother became popularly known as 'Harry'. He was easygoing and could make friends effortlessly. His personality was completely opposite to mine. Within a week in England, he started going to the pub with the landlord and the landlady. By the end of that week, he even started cooking curry in the kitchen and sharing it with them. He was a great cook, and the curry and rice were always delicious. We only possessed one plate to begin with and both of us had to eat our food from it. We would divide the food into equal parts by drawing a line across the middle. We went to see football matches when Blackburn Rovers were playing at home. We visited the local park, and I even went to a nightclub with him at his insistence. He loved dancing with the girls. And I could see he had become his old self, the brother I had known when he was going to secondary school.

Harry's training was at Queen's Park Hospital, whereas I was mainly based at Blackburn Royal Infirmary. He soon developed a friendship with three other Mauritian male nurses based there. The friendship blossomed, as all four of them, as well as Jimmy, had similar personalities. They loved going to the pub and drinking until closing time, and they loved chasing girls, particularly the young cadet nurses. They had compiled a list and were in some sort of competition to see who had most. I was totally averse to such pursuits and continued with my studies. I started spending more and more time in the hospital library, as Harry had become a great distraction to me.

Harry soon had a girlfriend, and I became angry with him for bringing her to our lodgings and kissing and hugging her in my presence. He had a wife and child in Mauritius. How could he forget them so easily?

'I am disgusted with you. You have been here only three months and have girlfriends. What about Neera?'

'She is not going to find out. I know you won't tell anybody in Mauritius about this.'

What was the point of telling anybody about my brother's selfish behaviour? We made an agreement that from that day onwards he would not bring any girl home while I was there in the same room.

Despite his many distractions, my brother managed to pass his final examination and qualified as a State Enrolled Nurse. I urged him on many occasions to enrol himself in evening classes to improve his qualifications. He already had two subjects at Cambridge School Certificate. With a further one subject at "O" level he could have completed his State Registered Nurse training and returned home and obtained a post as a qualified registered nurse. Instead, he chose to specialise in thoracic surgery at Baguley Hospital in Wythenshawe. To my great sadness he moved away from Blackburn leaving me behind in that dilapidated room.

I had little time to miss his absence, however, as I was busy preparing for my final State Registered Nurse examination. We all had to take the hospital examination as a mock preparation for the final. It was a momentous time of my life when I passed the mock examination with distinction and came out first in all the main papers including practical nursing. In the history of Blackburn Royal Infirmary, I was the first male nurse to be awarded first prize in nursing at a very pompous ceremony. I asked my landlord and landlady to accompany me to the ceremony. After, they took me to a pub. It was the first time I had a drink with them, despite living in the same house for over two years. I took the final examination in October 1969 and passed it at my first attempt. Jimmy, who was a year senior to me, had already failed his final twice. I'd been encouraging him to study with me and participate in various discussions on aspects of nursing care. I was delighted for him when he finally made it.

I was a proud man and wrote to Ma and my brother-in-law about my success. They urged me to return home. I was by now twenty-four years old, fully qualified and in possession of five GCE O Levels as I had passed my re-sit examination as Ma had predicted. I would easily obtain a job in Mauritius. My youngest sister sent me a photograph of a girl she thought would make a suitable bride for me. She had long hair, inviting brown eyes and looked beautiful. According to my younger sister, she was the only daughter of a rich family. Most importantly, she worked in a bank having passed her A Level examination. I was tempted to return to Mauritius, but I had other ideas.

In the meantime, I was offered a permanent job at the hospital on one of the male orthopaedic wards. I was now earning a good salary as a staff nurse and was able to save at least two thirds of my earnings. Orthopaedic nursing fascinated me. In the trauma unit, most of the patients were young victims of motorbike and car accidents, and I felt proud and fulfilled seeing them go home following a dreadful accident. I wanted to know more about the body's bones, muscles and joints. I decided that rather than go home, I would complete my Orthopaedic Certificate before settling down in Mauritius. It was only a one-year course, and I did not want to miss the opportunity to gain that renowned higher qualification. As I did not want to move far away from my brother, I managed to obtain a staff nurse post at Crumpsall Hospital, which allowed me to complete my Orthopaedic Certificate after one year of training. I would start on 1 April 1970, living in decent accommodation in the nurses' home.

I wrote to Ma and my brother-in-law about my intention. I assured them I would return home after this year of post-graduate training and settle down in Mauritius. I also promised that I would marry their chosen bride. It was a happy time for me. Everything I had planned I would be able to achieve. I wanted to save as much money as possible so that I could return home rich and well qualified.

Chapter Thirty

I settled into my new role as an orthopaedic student at Crumpsall Hospital quite easily. The hospital looked very dilapidated. It was a gigantic place with long corridors. All the wards were located on each side of the main three-storey building. In the past it had been a workhouse and some patients still referred to it as 'that workhouse building'. It was situated in the north of Manchester about six miles from the centre. There was a large Jewish community within walking distance of the hospital and many shops in the area sold Asian vegetables and a large variety of products.

I was offered a cosy place in the male nurses' residence just above the main kitchen. It was rather noisy during dining hours but it did not bother me too much. I had a bedroom and a sitting room that faced the front of the main building. It had a kitchen which was well stocked with the usual pots and pans and I was able to cook freely. For the first time, I felt able to cook curry and rice and eat it in my sitting room and was happy. I no longer felt constrained.

One day I was cooking chicken curry when a tall gentleman wearing a staff nurse's uniform walked into the kitchen.

'Ah, what a nice smell. What are you cooking?' he said in a strong Irish accent.

'Chicken curry and rice. Do you do a lot of cooking here?'

'Oh no. I normally eat in the dining room. I don't know much about cooking.'

He introduced himself as Morgan Johnson and I invited him to share some of the food. He loved my cooking, and from then on it became a habit when we were off together for me to cook curry and rice and enjoy the meal together. He always insisted he would do all the shopping and pay for it. We became great friends. Morgan's room was next to mine, and this helped consolidate our friendship. He worked in one of the male surgical wards as a senior staff nurse on the second floor of the building, while the orthopaedic wards were located on the ground floor.

Morgan owned a white Volkswagen Beetle and he would drive me around Manchester. He was Irish through and through and hated the English, even though most of his girlfriends were English. He was a religious Catholic and would take me to his religious groups thinking, perhaps, that one day he would convert me to Christianity. Although I was Hindu, I did not mind accompanying him and would sing hymns and get involved in various Christian activities, although the main thing that attracted me was the fact that at the end of each session, we would have tea and delicious cakes. The members of the group were equally friendly, and I would enjoy sharing with them my Mauritian experiences.

One lunchtime, about a month after my arrival, I was sitting by myself at a round table in the hospital canteen, when my deep meditation was suddenly interrupted by a soft voice.

'Are these chairs occupied?'

I looked up and saw three student nurses standing by my table, holding their trays and looking at me with bright, eager eyes. They were wearing deep blue uniforms and had their hair tied back and their fob watches neatly fastened on the left side of their chest.

The youngest looking of the three had asked the question.

'No.' I replied. 'Do sit down.'

The three students quickly scrambled to sit around me their plates full to overflowing. They started tucking in like ravenous animals as soon as they sat down, and hardly paid any attention to my presence. I looked at the youngest nurse, the one who had enquired about the empty seats, and felt an inner pang. She was pretty with a sharp nose, rather different from her two friends. I felt a nervous tension rising inside me. I had never experienced such a surge of strange feelings before. On and off she raised her face and looked at me, her green eyes gleaming. I thought her eyes were revealing something I could not figure out in that brief moment. Her smiling face looked inviting, friendly and sincere. She looked enchanting. I could not stop myself from looking at her, even the way she quickly forked her food. I had been in England for over three years and had always made a point of ignoring girls. But this girl had captivated me, and I could not explain what had happened to me.

I tentatively introduced myself as a staff nurse working in the Orthopaedic Unit.

'I'm Alison,' the youngest nurse replied. 'This is Mary and this is Sue. We're all degree students from the University of Manchester completing our third-year placement at the hospital.'

I had not heard of degree nursing. In the orthopaedic wards at Crumpsall Hospital only the third-year student nurses who were training for their general registration were allocated for practical experience. Orthopaedic wards were seen as a specialised unit.

'How different is degree nursing from the general nurse training?' I asked.

I was glad I raised that question; it delayed them vacating the table as Mary explained, giving me my first insight into degree nursing.

Alison kept giving me a friendly smile while cleaning up her plate. Her friends still had a few morsels on theirs, and they teased her for the way she ate.

'Do you work on the ward or in the community? I enquired, smiling at Alison.

It was apparent that Mary and Sue felt they were being left out of the conversation. Sue tentatively looked at Mary and raised her eyebrows asking what was going on. Mary shrugged her shoulders.

'We should be going, Alison,' she said abruptly. 'We're going to be late. Come on girls, Sister will be hopping mad. Do you remember what she did to us last time we were two minutes late?'

Mary pulled her chair out and stood up without looking at me, placed her used cutlery on the discarded tray and started making her way out of the canteen followed by Sue.

Alison slowly got up from her chair and gave me another sweet smile that showed her white teeth.

‘Oh, goodbye.’

I smiled and waved, following her with my eyes as she made her way out with her friends. She was short and slim, I guessed about five foot one or two in height. I kept looking, and without any further thought my glances fell on her shapely bottom, which gave a tiny swing to the left and right as she walked.

In my emotional bewilderment I had forgotten to ask the three friends the ward of their placement and wondered whether I would ever see them again.

That night I kept thinking of Alison. Up to that point of my life no girl had ever left a lasting impression on me. Her smiling face and beautiful eyes kept me awake most of the night. I was determined to find out more about her.

Earlier in the evening I had gone with Morgan to a spiritual meeting somewhere in the countryside. On our way to the meeting, I had spoken tentatively about Alison.

‘Morgan, I met a girl today.’

‘Yes, Jay? What about her?’

‘She is very pretty. Her name is Alison and I think she is a university student.’

‘Well, ask her out then.’

I did not know what to say. I had never directly asked a girl out.

‘Do you know her?’ I asked.

I knew Morgan was going out with a university student, but I did not know her name and had never seen her with him.

'Oh, yes. I know her. She works in the female ward on the same floor as mine. She seems to be a nice girl. But you can't trust these English girls, Jay. You have to be very careful.'

He beamed, and I left the conversation about Alison there, quite pleased I had been able to trace her. Next day I was having my lunch and Morgan was with me. While we were chatting, I saw Alison and Mary making their way to the staff sitting room. My heart started palpitating at the sight of her. I could not concentrate on what Morgan was telling me.

Then and there I tore a page from the pocket notebook I always carried with me and scribbled the following words: *Please, would you be able to meet me at 4 pm tomorrow in the staff sitting room of the Nurses' Home?*

I signed my name and folded the paper into quarters. I addressed it 'To Alison' and asked Morgan to hand it to her. He was reluctant at first, but with a bit of persuasion made his way towards Alison and handed her the note. He pointed towards me and Alison gave a surprised glance in my direction. I thought it was an encouraging sign. That night when I was restless in bed, I kept asking myself 'Oh God what happened to me?'

Chapter Thirty-One

That night I hardly slept. I kept tossing and turning in my bed. Alison kept featuring in various guises in my dreams. It was difficult to explain what had happened to me. I had hardly talked to her during that lunch break, yet her sweet smile and her friendly demeanour had left a deep impression on me. I just had to see her.

I asked my charge nurse whether I could leave early that afternoon for an important appointment. He accepted the excuse and let me go. I quickly had a shower, put on my best jacket and striped trousers and made my way to the sitting room. It was only half past three, but I could not wait to meet Alison. At precisely four o'clock Alison walked into the sitting room in her blue uniform. I stood in front of her and just looked at her without saying a single word. She looked dazzling, and her beautiful smile wrapped me in sheer delight: a moment I will always treasure.

We were both very young when we met. Alison was only twenty years old and I was twenty-four. Despite my age I was very naive and totally inexperienced with girls. There had been girls interested in me, like Sandra, Jeanette and some of the cadet nurses, but I was never serious with them. My upbringing in a small Hindu village had taught me that girls should always be respected. Arranged marriage was the norm. One never went out with a girl prior to getting married, and I had never heard of any boys or girls crossing this traditional boundary in our village. Although it was quite common to cross this boundary in the major towns, I was unaware of it at the time. I always thought that if a man went out with a girl, such a relationship should only lead to marriage. Otherwise, the girl's future would be ruined.

I was terrified on our first date. I had no idea what one did in the company of a girl. It felt very strange when I took Alison into the small Crumpsall Park that evening after work. It must have been about five o'clock. We strolled along the flower borders admiring the various types of roses and their beautiful colours. I did not know the name of any of the plants, but Alison had a good knowledge of them. She told me she had studied Botany at A Level. I thought Alison was clever and a very shrewd girl. She knew so many things of which I was totally ignorant. I was very impressed. After an hour's stroll in the park, Alison reminded me she had to catch her bus home. We quickly said goodbye at the bus stop and, in a flash, she was gone, leaving me standing, baffled, on the pavement. I had not even managed to hold her hand or ask her out again. I had no idea where she lived and came home rather deflated, wondering whether I would ever meet her again as I thought I had made a mess of everything.

For the next few weeks, I tried in vain to find Alison, for she seemed to have vanished into thin air. I went to the dining room at various times in search of her, but she never appeared. Morgan was on holidays for two weeks, so I could not ask for his help. In desperation I went to the ward where she had been working and spoke to the ward clerk.

'Good morning. I'm a staff nurse and I'm looking for the university student who was working on this ward.'

'She's gone. She's finished her placement on this ward.'

'How will I find out her next placement?'

'You have to go to the basement and talk to her clinical teacher.'

I was rather pleased with my detective work. At least I had some sort of lead. Within ten minutes I was in the basement. I had never gone there before. The corridor was very long, and I had entered it right in the middle. After glancing both the east and west, I made the choice of walking to the east. I did not know the clinical teacher's name nor did I know what she looked like. It was not until I went to the very end of the corridor that I found a sign on a door 'Clinical Teacher'. I gently knocked the door and to my surprise and delight a lady's voice answered.

'Come in.'

I quietly opened the door and immediately faced a rather obese lady sitting at a desk with red pen in her hand, obviously marking papers.

'Yes.'

'I'm a staff nurse from the Orthopaedic Ward. I am looking for a university student who was working on Blue Ward.'

She lifted her head and gave me a sympathetic look. 'What's her name?'

'Alison.'

'Ah, I know her. She's rather reserved. Are you her boyfriend?'

'Oh, no.'

‘All the university students are on holidays now. They won’t be back for another three weeks.’

The Clinical Teacher informed me with a broad smile that Alison would be placed on Delaunay’s Ward. I thanked her very much for the information and left her office a rather relieved man. I had not lost her.

It was awful waiting. I wondered many times why she hadn’t told me she was going on holidays when we met in that park. As her Delaunay’s Ward placement came nearer and nearer, I became convinced she did not like me. Otherwise, I thought, she would have told me of her next move.

University students usually worked straight shifts from half past seven in the morning until half past three in the afternoon. They were nearly always off over the weekend. The rest of the staff, including myself, often worked split, morning or afternoon shifts in rotation. Being an orthopaedic student, my two days off often fell during the week, so at first it was rather difficult to arrange a suitable time to seek Alison out.

My first attempt to meet her was roughly rebutted by the ward sister. I was not allowed to visit a nurse while she was on duty. Next day, being my day off, I went to the hospital florist and bought a single red rose. I wrapped it carefully and put a note with it, asking her to meet me along the corridor by the female changing room. I left the flower and the note with the ward clerk hoping she would hand them over to Alison.

Alison was waiting for me as I arrived at the rendezvous. My persistence had paid off. We soon became intimate friends. We went to parks, cinemas and even to a disco in the centre of Manchester. Just being with her made these the happiest days of my life. And although during my training I had to spend time at different sites to get a balanced clinical experience (like Oswestry where I learnt about the Charnley hip replacement), we managed to remain in touch with each other.

One day, while we were sitting in the park, Alison said her Mum and Dad, who lived in Wrexham wanted to meet me. I agreed to the visit, as my relationship with Alison was deepening and I felt it was appropriate they should see me in the flesh. I was equally curious to meet them. It was arranged that her father would collect me from Chester railway station and I'd stay the weekend at their place in Marford, just over six miles from the centre of Wrexham.

By then, I was quite au fait with British culture and knew what was expected of me. Still, I was terrified when my train approached Chester Station. I found that Mr Moat, Alison's father, was a real gentleman. Although rather reserved with me, he was pleasant and carried my luggage to his car. Alison and I sat in the back seat clutching each other's hands. On the way to their house, he kept looking at me in the rearview mirror. I wondered what he thought of me, a brown man, sitting by his beloved daughter.

Although, I had an anxious time at Alison's house, I thought my visit was a success. Alison's mum was exceptionally nice to me. She asked many questions about my family and particularly about my future plans. She also cooked some delicious food to satisfy my Indian palate. I met Alison's grandfather who was a very thin man. His left hand had been affected by polio and he had a bad habit of smoking cigarettes like a chimney. I also met David, Alison's eighteen-year-old brother who was studying for his A Levels at that time. I immediately sensed that David was not keen about my visit. I had bought a Motown record by the Supremes for him, and to my great surprise and disappointment he politely refused to accept my gift, clearly indicating that such music was not to his liking.

Until then, I had not realised that Alison's father was quite an important figure in Wrexham, being the town's treasurer, a prestigious position in the county. His polite, welcoming manners impressed me. He did not ask me many questions, except to ascertain whether I was serious in my relationship with his only daughter. He impressed on me that he did not want his daughter to be hurt. I concluded from my short visit that the Moat family was fairly well off, considering the size of their detached house, with its spacious rooms and modern furniture.

After six months of hectic courtship, we got engaged. To mark the occasion, I bought Alison a beautiful engagement ring, which she chose at a jeweller's shop in the centre of Manchester.

It was clear that my blossoming relationship with Alison was leading to marriage. However, I still had some lingering doubts about whether I was really serious in marrying her. I was a brown man, an Indian Mauritian with a very different upbringing. I thought about children, and the impact it might have on them coming from a mixed marriage. I was scared of what the future might bring, and because of my uncertainty and confusion I kept our engagement a secret from Ma, my brother-in-law and my sisters. I had promised my family I would return to Mauritius after my orthopaedic training and marry the Hindu girl they had chosen for me. I was in a real dilemma and did not know what to do. By marrying Alison, I was going to break my promise and let down the girl who had, until then, been waiting for me for nearly a year. But most importantly, I felt I was rejecting my Hindu culture and all its traditions. Alison had a Christian background. Although she was not a practicing Christian, she had been brought up in a totally different culture. Despite being intelligent, she had no concept of my background. There was nobody I could turn to for advice.

Chapter Thirty-Two

By the beginning of 1972 I had been engaged for over two years and had still failed to inform my family in Mauritius. Even my brother Harry, who was working at Wythenshawe Hospital, had no knowledge of my engagement to Alison. I had successfully completed my orthopaedic nursing course and had obtained a job as a charge nurse at Stockport Infirmary. I was under great pressure, because Alison expected to get married and I was still lingering and making excuses.

In the end, to resolve my dilemma once and for all, I decided to pay my first visit to Mauritius after nearly five years in England. When I mentioned to Alison about my impending visit she understood and wanted to come with me. I declined, arguing it would be easier for me to explain to my family about our engagement. She lent me her best suitcase and also loaned me about £50, as I had run out of money after having paid for the aeroplane ticket and buying gifts for my family. I was taken aback by the level of trust she placed in me. I knew I was deceiving her as I had decided I would settle down in Mauritius and marry the Hindu girl of my own caste who my family had chosen for me.

When I said goodbye to Alison, I knew that most probably I would never see her again. I was torn between the wishes of my family, my promise to them and my personal feeling. I dearly loved and cared for Alison. I knew deep in my heart that I really wanted to marry her, but I just could not cross that nuptial boundary.

In the five years I had been away, Mauritius had changed considerably. She obtained her full independence from the mother country in 1968. There were many white tourists at Plaisance Airport, and among them I noticed a few mixed married couples with children. The majority of my old village friends were still working as labourers, but others were employed in the hotels that were mushrooming all along the beaches. The standard of living had improved dramatically and nearly all the villagers had brick houses with indoor toilets, electricity and a television. Many even had cars on their driveway.

I stayed in Triolet with my mother and sister-in-law, Neera and her five-year-old daughter, Devianee. The child looked sad and bewildered, and naturally had no idea who I was. Ma and Neera looked thin and malnourished. The front garden was overgrown and everywhere I looked there were signs of neglect, which horrified me. Their unhappiness touched the very core of my heart. I knew Harry was enjoying himself in England. He had several girlfriends and had even gone to Spain on holiday with one of them. I was angry with myself. If I had not facilitated Harry's journey to England the family would not have suffered. What was the point of him being employed in a different country and earning a good salary, when his wife and only child were suffering? Neera and their daughter needed him. I knew I had made a great mistake.

'Oh God, what have I done?' I kept asking myself.

I decided the situation had to be remedied. The next day I went to the Ministry of Health of Mauritius and enquired about the possibility of Harry obtaining a full-time job as a nurse. I was assured he had a good chance of obtaining a job as an enrolled nurse. I completed an application form on his behalf, and having falsified his signature left the completed form at the Ministry.

In the meantime, Deomatee, my youngest sister, was harassing me about my impending marriage with the Mauritian girl. She thought I had come to Mauritius to marry the girl of her choosing, and she urgently wanted me to visit the girl's family. I managed to postpone the visit for another week.

This gave me at least two weeks to reflect upon my relationship with Alison. I found that the attitudes of Mauritians had changed. The improved standard of living had made them very materialistic. Most of the gifts I had brought with me were not enthusiastically received by my family. They felt that they looked cheap, which was true as I didn't have the money to buy expensive gifts. Both of my sisters looked better off than me. They had expensive furniture in their houses, dressed in expensive clothes and had started eating meat, which was a sign of wealth. The village customs were already weakening fast, and respect for the Elders was waning. Most of the young boys were fully employed. Instead of working in the fields, they preferred to toil regular hours in the big clothing and woollen factories that were opening all over Mauritius, financed by China and India. The youngsters had cash in their hands and seemed freed from domination by their parents. Even Ma was asking why I was not wearing a suit and tie, even though the heat was sweltering. I was being encouraged to hire a car rather than travel by bus.

It was obvious my family had adjusted to life without me there. Harry needed to be there more than me. I felt I had become an outsider. After three weeks in Mauritius, I started becoming dissatisfied with all aspects of Mauritian life. By this time my application for a staff nurse post at one of the local hospitals had been accepted, and I was due to commence within four weeks. My plane ticket would expire in three weeks. I had to make a decision. Should I settle down in Mauritius or return to England and marry Alison?

I finally decided I did not want to settle in Mauritius. After nearly six years in England, I had changed. Unconsciously, I had assimilated the British way of life. I was bitterly missing Alison. I wanted to return to England and marry her. However, I was still unwilling to tell anybody in Mauritius about my feelings for Alison. During the last week of my stay, I told Deomatee it would be a waste of time visiting the girl's family, as it was not my intention to marry any Mauritian girls at that moment. Of course, the whole family was disappointed and angry with me. Eventually, my impending marriage with the Mauritian girl was forgotten, and I returned to England as a bachelor.

Chapter Thirty-Three

On my return to England, I immediately went to see Harry at his hospital. I informed him how Mauritius had changed to the better and how I had managed to find a job for him. For the first time I also told him about my relationship with Alison.

'You must return home, Harry, immediately. Neera and your daughter miss you very much. They are in a desperate situation. You now have a guaranteed job as an enrolled nurse and can lead a comfortable life. There will also be an opportunity for you to complete your General Nursing course after one year of further training.'

'What about you?' he asked.

'I am a single man. I do not have the same responsibility as you have. I'll stay here a bit longer.'

'Are you going to marry that white English girl?'

'I might. I have not decided yet.'

I was still dithering about marrying Alison. The thought of marriage to an English girl still caused me heartache. I was very conscious I was going to lose my Hindu identity, and more importantly, upset my family in Mauritius. On the other hand, Alison was pressing me to make up my mind. We had now been engaged for over three years, but I still thought marriage was only a very distant possibility.

In the end, Alison decided to play her final card. She told me in no uncertain terms that she would not see me any more unless I came up with a firm date for our marriage. But I'd always had a very stubborn and unforgiving nature, and her ultimatum was counterproductive. I thought at last I had a good excuse to break my engagement. I tried to forget her by devoting my time to studying GCE O Level Chemistry at Stockport College in the evening. I also seriously thought that I would after all return to Mauritius with Harry.

It was during this upsetting period I decided to visit Harry again at his hospital residence in Wythenshawe. So, one weekend, I just turned up. I wanted to meet my brother and talk to him face to face and share with him my problems. I thought that he would help me to reach a solution. Instead, when I knocked on his door, there was no response. I tried several times and my persistence at last paid off.

In the end Harry opened his door. I cursed him for making me wait outside and pushed myself in as I had always done. The sight of a blonde girl in his room made my blood boil. I had seen her on a previous meeting. She was a beautiful, slim girl with deep blue eyes who worked as a receptionist on one of the wards. The image of Neera and Devianee flashed in front of my eyes. They were suffering in Mauritius, and here was Harry enjoying himself without any qualms. I lost my temper and told him what I thought of him. I also told the girl about Harry's marriage and his five-year-old daughter.

I now believe it was unforgivable on my part to divulge his secret to his girlfriend. But what could have I done? I was angry at his total lack of empathy for his family. Harry knew full well that the Ministry of Health of Mauritius had confirmed his post as a nurse. But it appeared he had ignored the letter I'd sent him. I decided Harry had to leave England and go back to Neera where he really belonged. During that week, before my anger cooled down, I booked a seat with British Airways and handed him the ticket. I also gave him £200 in cash to help him settle in Mauritius. Within three weeks of the encounter Harry was on his way home. He left his cosy life in England cursing me. As I had promised, he obtained the nursing post. It was extremely difficult for him to resettle in Mauritius, but at least I'd managed to save his marriage with Neera. I know he never forgave me for my dreadful action. He wanted to remain in England and marry the girl. I had destroyed his dream, whereas I stayed on in England. I could have accompanied my brother, as I too had secured a post in one of the hospitals. But I never told him that.

As a charge nurse at Stockport Infirmary, I was comfortably off and had a flat in Heaton Moor that was only a ten-minute walk from where Alison lived. But I had not seen her for a while since she gave me her final ultimatum and had started getting the idea that my relationship with her had finished for good. By now Harry had left England for nearly three months and had stopped sending any money for their upkeep. I knew that Harry was fairly well paid and hoped at least normality would return to his life. At this point I had no idea what was the best direction I should take to shape my future. But at the back of my mind, I still wanted to return to Mauritius and settle down.

One evening, I was in my flat listening to some music when my relaxing evening was disturbed by a gentle knock on my flat door. It was my landlady's daughter, who informed me there was a girl outside who wanted to see me. I thought it was the Irish staff nurse from my ward who had started showing some interest in me, as I had given her my address. I jumped from my bed and dashed downstairs to greet her. To my great surprise it was not the staff nurse; it was Alison.

She ran to me and hugged me and started crying. 'I missed you, Jay,' she sobbed, tears streaming down her face.

I stood there, dumbfounded, clasped in her arms. 'I missed you too, Alison. But pride prevented me from approaching you. I am so glad you came to me.'

I held her tight, raised her head gently towards me and kissed her. Perhaps it was the first time I ever kissed her in public, as no doubt Mrs Lord, my landlady, and her daughter were watching from behind the curtains.

I agreed then and there that it was time we got married, and the next day I went to the Stockport Registry Office and fixed a date for the wedding to be held in June 1974. That weekend, Alison and I visited her parents and sought their permission to marry. They were reservedly pleased. Her father asked me many questions, particularly about future plans, the ceremony and the guest list. I had no idea how to answer. I had not thought about those issues. That afternoon, Alison's Mum called me to her bedroom while Alison was away on an errand with her father. She made me sit down beside her.

'Jay, as you know Alison is my only daughter. I hope you will keep her happy.'

'Of course, I will, Mrs Moat,' I promised.

'May I ask you a favour?' she said quietly, looking straight at me.

I waited patiently. I could tell she was hesitating.

Suddenly she burst into tears. 'I always wanted my girl to be married in a church. Can you do that Jay?'

'I am a Hindu, Mrs Moat. I cannot marry in a church. Besides, we have already booked the Registry Office.'

'Think again, Jay. Please.'

I was touched by Mrs Moat's plea. Following few days reflection, I decided that Alison and I should get married in an Anglican church. I laid aside my precious Hindu principles, and we booked to be married in the beautiful Saint Elizabeth's Church in Reddish, Stockport on 10 August 1974.

It was a beautiful day. We had at least forty guests. Perhaps ten of those were from my side, including my friend Raj and his wife from Blackburn and colleagues from my workplace. I had informed my family of my impending marriage, but nobody could attend because of the prohibitive cost, so Mr and Mrs Lord (my landlord and landlady) cheerfully acted as my parents.

I was dressed in a brown suit, shirt, tie and brown shoes that still had the sale label attached to the sole. Alison was dressed in a white satin wedding dress, which she had sewn herself over many weeks, and a short see-through veil. Her hair was adorned with white flowers aptly symbolising her innocence, honesty and sublime beauty. She looked like a princess. I was, although petrified, the happiest man on the planet.

The vicar understood my faith, and during the ceremony he stressed the similarity of Hindu and Christianity wedding vows, for which I was very thankful.

The reception, which ran very smoothly, was organised and paid for by Mr Moat. Alison and I cut the three-layered cake and I delivered my well-rehearsed speech, which had been jointly written by five of my patients. We spent our honeymoon in Scotland touring the Western side of the country in Alison's little grey Mini. We mainly stayed in bed and breakfast places. I was not insured to drive the car so was tasked with navigating the way. I was a rotten map reader. Most of the time we lost our way, which led to heated arguments. We had taken our portable kettle with us and a gas burner, and at various points in the day we would stop the car, sometimes in a lay-by and sometimes in a field, and brew our precious tea and eat our sandwiches. We felt free and on top of the world. It was wonderful to be with Alison twenty-four hours a day. I wondered why it had taken me four years to marry her. Oh, how sweet it is to remember those joyous moments. I knew I was a very lucky man to have married a girl like Alison and thanked God that I had been blessed with such a bride.

By leaving Mauritius to live in the mother country, I had broken many Hindu principles as well as promises I had given to my Dadi, Ma, my dear brother-in-law and my sisters. When I married Alison, I felt the last remnants of my Hindu culture were torn to pieces. In my childhood I suffered neglect, starvation, discrimination and heart-breaking humiliation, and had to be shunted from one house to another so that I could get an education. Despite the hardships, I was determined to succeed and improve my situation and that of my family. I can proudly say I achieved this. But my conscience still nags me that, for the sake of ambition, I broke promises I had given in sincere faith.

However, I still feel that the price of my success in my Mother Country was enormous. I had to learn to conform fairly quickly to the British ways of living. My marriage with Alison smoothed that process greatly. Before my marriage I was often addressed as 'Paki' by people in the streets. I was scared to walk on my own. But after our marriage, somehow, her presence gave me protection against overt discrimination. I became more confident during my assimilation of British cultures and customs. I felt all along that I did not see myself as an immigrant but a fully-fledged British citizen. Was my conformity a price worth paying I asked myself many times?

Epilogue

Part One

'Nana, come and play with me.'

Mila, my four-year-old Nateen *(*granddaughter), is holding my hand and pulling me off my reclining chair, while I am in vain trying to get my afternoon nap. Hiro, my one-year-old Natee (grandson) is playing nearby with his toys.

I am now seventy-four years old and fully retired following a varied career as nurse, senior lecturer at the University of Surrey, solicitor, barrister and PhD graduate. I was called to the Bar after having studied part time for two years whilst in fulltime work as a Senior Nurse Tutor.

I desperately wanted to be a lawyer because I had seen so many injustices metered out during my nursing career. While we were in Stockport, I studied for my LL.B Degree part-time at the University of Manchester. The courses were held on two evenings from 6 pm to 9 pm and a full day on Saturday. Both Anita and Nadine were very young and Alison was working full time as a Health Visitor.

It was very hard going but my determination and experience of studying on my own in the Central Library of Mauritius helped me along. I had to get up at four every morning to complete my course. I am afraid that during this time I hardly played with the children. I have been blamed by my girls many times for neglecting them when they needed me most. But I was too focused in my determination to complete my law degree. Despite all the odds I obtained my LL.B degree with a 2.2 pass.

In the 1990's the Bar Professional Training Course (BPTC) was only held in London. Despite my greatest dilemma of leaving my family behind in Stockport, I decided to move to Guildford on my own, having obtained a Lecturer's post at the University of Surrey. I found myself a bedsit accommodation. As well as starting a new post, I enrolled myself on a two-year part-time BPTC in London. The course was held on Monday evenings from 6 to 9 pm and on Saturday and Sundays

It was a very demanding course. I was in uncharted territory. Besides preparing my University lectures I had to keep up with my Bar studies. We were rigorously tested nearly every two weeks. Any failure meant being thrown out of the course without a second thought. I spent half of the night and early morning engrossed in my studies. My life revolved around my studies. I was very fortunate because as the University of Surrey was running an LL.B course its library was full of up to date law books. This helped me to research on current statute law and common law cases.

As part of the course, it was a mandatory requirement that every Bar student should become a member of an Inns of Court. I became a member of the Middle Temple which meant that I had to travel to London on *'twelve Dinner'* occasions to have posh evening meals with my Inns of Court Supervisor whose role was to support me and guide me in my studies. Nearly every week he arranged for me to sit with an eminent practicing judge whom I could ask any probing questions about the complexities of being a Barrister and his triumphant cases in court. It was an exciting period although very taxing on energy and my finance.

After three months Alison managed to sell our Stockport house and moved to Guildford with the children. At last, after horrendous sacrifice on both our parts, we were reunited as a family. I placed Anita in a private girls' school whilst Nadine attended a renowned local primary school. Alison managed to obtain a Health Visitors position. We rented a three-bed room house in Frimley until we thought we could afford to buy a house of our own as properties in Surrey were nearly twice as expensive as Stockport.

After two years study I managed to pass my Bar examinations. My success was a miracle in itself as more than twenty per cent of my friends failed. There was a rumour flying around at that time that failing up to twenty-five per cent of the students was a deliberate ploy to screen out the less able prospective Barristers. Although I was very happy with my success, I was warned by my supervisor that passing the Bar examination was only the first step towards becoming a Barrister.

My next step was to seek a Chamber which would take me for Pupillage. I had to compete with Eton, Oxford and Cambridge graduates. I learnt that students with a known family background were more likely to obtain a pupillage. On many occasions I was told my skin was the wrong colour. It was a futile attempt. Despite repeated applications I was rejected. I did not receive a single interview. It was a difficult moment in my life. I cursed myself for being a member of an ethnic minority without a good family connection. Still my realisation that I would never practice as a Barrister was very difficult to swallow and left me shocked by the treatment I received.

Although disappointed at failing to secure a pupillage, my success at the bar helped me gain a senior Lecturer's position. Because of my legal and nursing background I was often asked to lecture on subjects of law to students across the various University Faculties. I was elected to the Ethical Committee, a prestigious position, and started rubbing shoulders with the top university professors and hospital consultants.

It was during this time that I was advised that if I were to obtain a PhD degree, I had a great chance to become a professor and obtain a chair at the University. I just could not let this unique chance pass by. The thought of the village sugarcane man becoming a professor fired my imagination.

In the year 2000, under the guidance of a well-known PhD supervisor I embarked on a three-year part-time research study. My research used an ethnographic methodology to address the issues of privacy of the person, patients' expectations and the level of intrusions by health professionals within the NHs hospital ward settings. I completed my study in the year 2004 which enabled me to gain my PhD.

Following my research, I published various papers on the 'Privacy and Dignity of Patients within our NHS hospitals.'

My publications and recommendations were well acclaimed. I started receiving invitations throughout Europe, America and Asia to explain my research findings and help professionals improve privacy and dignity of their patients in their respective health settings.

I was a proud and very happy man, at the top of my career and ready for the Chair of Professorship when, out of the blue in the year 2005, my mother was taken seriously ill in Mauritius. I had always suffered guilt for leaving Mauritius and, when I heard about her illness, I knew it was my duty to share the burden of looking after her. I resigned my position from the University of Surrey and my wife and I spent six months at a time in Mauritius for nearly six years to give Ma the best care that was humanely possible until she died in 2011.

Part Two

Throughout all my personal pursuits, Alison remained my backbone along our tortuous journey. We are still happily married and growing old together. We made our nest in a semi-detached bungalow in Guildford, a much sought-after area of leafy Surrey. We are proud of two beautiful girls: Anita, who was born in Scotland, now forty-one years old, married to Matt and settled in Bristol, and Nadine, who is thirty-seven years old, married to Max and living in Brighton with their two children, Mila and Hiro. In 2020 I bought a flat as a second home in Brighton so that we could spend more time with our grandchildren. Mila and Hiro come and stay with us when we are in Brighton, and we have a great time together.

Following our marriage in 1974, Alison and I moved to different places in the United Kingdom – Scotland, Nantwich, Stockport, and Guildford – as I sought promotion and in the quest for further qualifications. We also made several visits to Mauritius, both as a couple and with the children. During our second visit to Mauritius, when we had two-year-old Anita with us, Ma insisted we had to be properly married.

'You are living in sin, Jaysingh. A Hindu marriage will cleanse your body.'

'But Ma, I am already married and we have a child.'

It was fruitless arguing with her. We consented to be married in accordance with the Hindu custom and practice, as long as the ceremony was held in the presence of only the close family circle and focused on the blessings of a pundit and the relevant gods. Ma was very happy with this arrangement. During the ceremony we were also blessed by my sisters and my brother-in-law Bissoon, although by then my dearest brother-in-law had passed away. Everyone took great pride in performing the Aarti. After the short ceremony, we had a celebratory dinner full of laughter and great Indian jokes from Bissoon. It was a memorable occasion, and I was glad and felt very proud to have respected the wishes of Ma and my family. The Hindu marriage was a great stepping stone to integration into the family circle following our mixed marriage.

Despite leading a successful life in England, I was not really happy to settle there for good. I was not comfortable with the British culture. I thought children had too much freedom and was alarmed at the lack of morality among teenagers, particularly the way teenagers could pick and choose a partner for both short and long-term relationships without the consent of their parents and the way premarital sex and cohabitation had become the norm. I was convinced that such uncontrolled freedom was a big factor in the poor educational outcomes and the high divorce rate among the younger generations.

I was very unhappy at the thought of our children growing up in such a tainted society. I became more and more convinced that our children would be better off being brought up in a Hindu society where, with parental guidance, the exposure to a disciplined culture would, I thought, benefit them educationally and morally.

In April 1992, when Anita was fourteen years old and Nadine ten, I decided to uproot my family and return to Mauritius to live, despite the girls being settled at their schools and with their friends. At that time Anita was attending a private school in Guildford and Nadine was at primary school. I had bought myself a shop and a house in Mauritius, and thought that with the help of Bissoon I would make a successful shopkeeper. I was confident Alison could obtain a post as a nurse in one of the hospitals. We left our secure jobs, sold our house and shipped all our contents. On arrival, I placed Anita in one of the best state schools and Nadine in a private school.

After a few weeks in Mauritius, I started noticing the true colours of my close relatives. My dream of running the shop successfully was shattered, as Bissoon showed great reluctance to give me any help or support. In fact, my sister and Bissoon became very aggressive. I had bought the shop when Bissoon had problems with his brothers. I could not bear the thought of seeing Bissoon unemployed, and so had appointed him as manager with a forty per cent share while I made arrangements to move to Mauritius. This re-established his pride and confidence and he became a changed man. He used his charm and expertise in the import business and very soon the shop became a popular place for customers, as it was well stocked with goods from China, India and Indonesia.

During my various visits to Mauritius, I had warned them of my impending desire to settle there and run the shop business on my own. Throughout this discussion Bissoon had assured me he would share his knowhow when I took over. But I don't think they believed I would ever leave my cosy English life and well-paid university post to be a shopkeeper. So, instead of being welcomed with open arms, mistrust and jealousy awaited us and our relationship broke down to such an extent that my sister and Bissoon stopped talking to us and we were not welcome in their house.

I had a similar problem with Harry. I had bought some land and, in my absence, Harry had enjoyed all the profits from it for many years. While I was in England I never asked for a share of the proceeds. But he too, to my great consternation, adopted a similar posture to Bissoon and became very aggressive when I raised questions relating to this land that was, in fact, mine.

Besides, I soon realised the society I left behind in 1966 had changed completely. As I indicated previously tourism had become the main industry and the citizens had become wealthier and materialistic: nearly every household having a television and a car. The Elders were no longer treated with dignity and respect. People were so busy leading their own lives that they had no time to care for their elderly parents, and so nursing homes had mushroomed throughout the Island. These unfortunate elderly relatives were seen as a hindrance to self-development and freedom.

One day, when I returned home from the shop, tired and exasperated having not sold a single item all day, I was faced with a tearful Nadine.

'I want to go home.'

‘But this is our home, Nadine.’

‘The teacher hit me hard today.’

‘Why did he hit you?’

‘Because I couldn’t answer his questions in French. He has now moved me to the back row. I want to go home, Daddy, to my proper school.’

After meeting the teacher and the headmaster, it became apparent that corporal punishment was rife in schools. And since most of the teaching was in French, both Nadine and Anita were having great difficulties in coping with the content of the curricula.

I had not realised until that day that my children were greatly traumatised by the culture shock. I had been blind and selfish. Anita had become very withdrawn. Being a fourteen-year-old teenager, she missed her English friends more than Nadine. Anita, in her previous school was near the top of the class in all her subjects. Here, she was struggling in the lower third. And both of them had problems in making friends, as they were struggling to grapple with the Creole language.

After six months, I concluded I had made a horrible mistake in uprooting my family from their place of birth. I could not bear the thought of my children suffering any longer because of my desire to bring them up in a Hindu culture. We had no friends, and the rejection of my family was the final straw.

My total failure as a shopkeeper did not help our situation. In April of that year, I leased out the shop and we all returned to the mother country where we once again made a sweet home for our loving children. It had been a dream of mine to settle in Mauritius, but the society had changed so much since I had left in 1966, and so had I, that it was impossible to build a happy nest for us.

It was difficult to rebuild our life in the UK, but I was lucky enough to get my old post back at the university and Alison found a new one. Anita and Nadine returned to their old schools, and in due course both of them achieved great success both at university and in employment.

I have never forgotten my roots though. I visit Mauritius at least once a year and thereby maintain regular contact with my relatives. Our relationships have now greatly improved, and all bitterness of the past is forgotten. I lost my younger sister and Beau-frère through terminal illnesses, and Ma and more recently my dear brother Harry through old age. I still have Janee, my older sister who lives with her daughter, Madvi.

I was sitting in my conservatory the other day, reflecting on the different episodes in my life, when Mila pulled me from my reclining chair:

'Nana, you are not playing with us.'

I looked at Hiro and Mila, and prayed to God these innocent children would never face the hardships I had encountered in my journey through life.

And I reminisced:

As I lie in my soft reclining leather chair,
Having had a sumptuous Sunday feast,
I reflect on my life with a bellyful of pride.

Tears of joy trickle down my cheeks.
I know I have everything
That any human could dream of:
Such luxury and my delightful family to support me.

My achievements baffle me at times.
Am I the very man with the same name,
Who cut sugarcane in the searing heat,
Thrown out of school in disgrace,
Shunted from house to house and place to place?

But, within two score years I am completely changed.
Could it be my determination, my unfaltering ambition and faith,
My Karma, my thirst for knowledge and self-improvement?

I believe the true reason lies
In the fear of failure and loss of face,
Of letting down my Dadi,
Her principles and teaching,
And returning to my roots as a failure.

After a while Mila got tired of playing with her toys. She rushed to me and sat on my lap. 'Nana, can you tell me the sugarcane story again?'

Glossary of words in Hindi and Bhojpuri

Aarti – Hindu blessing

Beta - son. It can also be used as an elder calling a younger person.

Betee / Beti – daughter.

Bhaya – brother

Bhojpuri – a Hindi dialect (and Indo-Aryan language) commonly spoken in the western Bihar, India, where most of the indentured labourers in Mauritius came from.

Bhowjee – sister-in-law

Bomri – dried fish

Chachee – any woman in the village who was not related to one's family.

Chacha – male elder.

Chhetri – A Hindu caste, of 'warriors and rulers', who are believed to possess qualities of heroic mind, resourcefulness, courage and generosity. Members of the Chhetri caste always have a forename ending with the suffix 'singh'.

Didi - sister

Dadi – paternal grandmother.

Dhoti – a garment worn by male Hindus, consisting of a piece of material tied around the waist and extending to cover most of the legs.

Gateau Piments – chilli dhal fritters.

Hanumanji / Hanuman – one of the central characters of the Hindu epic, Ramayana. He is regarded to be the son of the Wind-God, Vayu.

Kirtan - a call-and-response style song or chant, with roots in the Vedic anukirtana tradition, that is set to music.

Mowsee – female cousin

Nagri – a term for a hamlet in Mauritius.

Natee – grandson.

Pioche –a draw hoe (farming tool).

Pugree - a light turban worn in India.

Puja / pooja – a worship ritual performed by Hindus, Buddhists and Jains.

Pundit – a term of respect for a wise person.

Roti – flat bread

Sona – term of endearment meaning 'golden boy.'

Vaishya – A Hindu caste, who in theory are merchants and farmers.

Author's Biography – Jay Woogara

Jay Woogara was born during the British Colonial rule of Mauritius into a poverty-stricken Hindu family. His father died when he was three years old leaving his Dadi (paternal grandmother) and Ma with four children all under age of ten.

The majority of the villagers were labourers and the men, women and children worked for the French white farmers. The Hindu caste system predominated, and discrimination in favour of the Creole Christians was rife.

From an early age Jay was determined to shake off the shackle of poverty and, through education, reach a level playing field.

Despite working in the sugarcane fields and being thrown out of fee-paying secondary school, he succeeded in gaining three GCE's Ordinary Level which enabled him to gain entrance into England in 1966 and to train as a nurse.

In spite of racial discrimination, he climbed the promotion ladder as a nurse teacher and later a senior University lecturer.

Since his hope was always to see fairness and justice for the patients and ethnic minority group alike, he studied law. After being called to the bar, he embarked on lecturing in the field of clinical negligence to doctors, nurses and other health workers.

During the years 2000 – 2004 Jay undertook research as part of his PhD to determine the extent to which health practitioners respect the dignity and privacy of patients in the hospital. Key aspects of his recommendations have been implemented throughout NHS settings

In 2014 he was elected as a Governor at Royal Surrey County Hospital. In that capacity he helped to shape various health policies. He also ensured that the Directors were held accountable for their actions.

Palewell Press

Palewell Press is an independent publisher handling poetry, fiction and non-fiction with a focus on books that foster Justice, Equality and Sustainability. The Editor can be reached on enquiries@palewellpress.co.uk